PATRICK J. BRENNAN

Full-Cycle Youth Evangelization

A Resource for Youth Ministers

FRIENDSHIP
LEADERSHIP
ACCEPTANCE
MINISTRY
EDUCATION

TABOR®
PUBLISHING

Allen, Texas

*T*hanks to Dawn Mayer Melendez, who actualized much of this with me, to Timothy O'Connell, who allows us to teach this at the Institute of Pastoral Studies, to Kathy Dziekanowski, who typed the manuscript, and to the many parishes and young people with whom I have worked.

Send all inquiries to:
Tabor Publishing
200 East Bethany Drive
Allen, Texas 75002-3804

Printed in the United States of America

ISBN 0-7829-0386-X

1 2 3 4 5   97 96 95 94 93

Contents

For Justin Brennan
and Stan Thomas,
both forever young.

Introduction

One of this country's larger dioceses has over three hundred parishes; yet only about forty of these parishes have youth ministers. The same situation can be found in many other dioceses throughout the United States. I fear this lack of investment will come back to bite us as a Church. Already, many young people are leaving. Increasingly, they are not tied into a Church, or they are attending evangelical churches. Forty years ago, Pierre Liegé, the founder of the modern evangelical movement, lamented the "graying" of the Church in Europe. The same thing is beginning to happen here. Without our young people, we will become a Church of the middle-aged and the old.

This simple book is a plea for long-term, dogged commitment to the evangelization and pastoral care of our adolescents and young adults. As a Church, we need to devote energy, innovation, and attention to a precious resource—our young people.

I know that vibrant, inclusive youth ministry can take place, for I have experienced it. I offer in these pages a vision of how to do such ministry, along with some pastoral wisdom I have gathered over the years. This vision is called FLAME—an acronym for Friendship, Leadership, Acceptance, Ministry, and Education—the five components of full-cycle youth evangelization. If these pages move even one person to work in ministry with young people, I will be happy. I will be even happier if ecclesial authorities, pastors, and pastoral workers wake up to both the crisis and the opportunity that youth present to the Church.

Patrick J. Brennan
Institute of Pastoral Studies
Loyola University Chicago
January 1993

1

The Dynamics of Youth

I see no help for our people if they are dependent on the frivolous youths of today, for all young people are reckless beyond words. . . . When I was a boy, we were taught to be discreet and respectful of elders; but the present youngsters are exceedingly 'wise' and impatient of restraint." These words could have been spoken by a parent or teacher today. But, in fact, they were written over two thousand years ago by Hesiod, a Greek poet. Hesiod's sentiments were echoed five hundred years later by Aristotle, a Greek philosopher, who spoke of youth as a time when desire overcomes the rational.

In the days of Hesiod and Aristotle, most people died in their thirties. Then, the term "youth" referred strictly to adolescents—people in their teen years. Today, because the average human lifespan is close to eighty, the term "youth" includes a much broader group. The category "young people" encompasses both teenagers and young adults—people from thirteen to forty.

Despite the fact that the definition of youth itself has changed, young people down through the ages have often been described by stereotypes. For example, young people have traditionally been characterized by extremes of emotion. In their intellectual, emotional, relational, and moral searching, they are described as being "in conflict with" the adult world. As the twentieth-century psychoanalyst Anna Freud observed, it is "normal" for a young person to be inconsistent and unpredictable—both to fight and to accept impulses, to ward them off and to be overrun by them. It is not unusual for youths simultaneously to love and to hate their parents, to revolt against them and to be dependent on them. One minute, young people can be idealistic, artistic, generous, and unselfish; the next minute, they can be just the opposite: self-centered, egotistical, and calculating.

Other traditional views have maintained that young people rarely reflect sufficiently on the possible dangerous results of their decisions and behaviors. They are often, in a word, nonreflective (although they have the capacity to be reflective, as Piaget, Fowler, and Kohlberg attest). Young people tend to be argumentative, but beneath their facade of bravado is an undertow of insecurity. They also have a tendency toward polar mood swings, often getting trapped for periods in bouts of loneliness. Personal hurt is not overcome easily. The young person who believes he or she can "go it alone" often retreats to parents for assistance. For the average young person, peer groups and school friends replace family, to some degree, as primary relationships.

A New View of Adolescence

The previous descriptions generically sum up the way older people have viewed younger people. Only recently, because of the pioneer work of psychologist Erik Erikson, have such views begun to change. As is now popularly known, Erikson saw human life as developing or evolving in eight stages. According to Erikson's epigenetic theory, the more advanced stages of human development build upon earlier ones. These stages are based on conflicts and their resolution.

The first of Erikson's stages (infancy) is based on the conflict between trust and mistrust. The infant moves toward trust or mistrust largely through interaction with his or her parents.

The second stage (post-infancy) is characterized by the conflict between autonomy and shame/doubt. The frequent "no" spoken by the two-year-old is the precursor of the adolescent's rebellion.[1]

---

[1] John Bradshaw has refashioned the traditional understanding of original sin to "original shame." Because of original shame, a child (and, later, an adolescent moving toward adulthood) develops a shameful, distrustful outlook on life.

The third stage (preschool) is characterized by the conflict between initiation and guilt. Again, parental interaction dictates whether the child values and practices risk-taking or hangs back in pseudo-guilt.

The fourth stage (early school years) presents the conflict between industry and inferiority. An industrious child is cooperative and relationally involved with peers and school authorities. A child with an inferiority complex does not cooperate and remains aloof.

The fifth stage (adolescence) is characterized by the conflict between identity and identity confusion.[2] This stage is the hinge of life. The teenager recapitulates all that has gone on before in his or her development, while pushing onward to the adult stages of life.[3]

The sixth stage (young adulthood) is characterized by the conflict between intimacy and isolation. The challenge of young adult development is to achieve healthy, mutual relationships and friendships that exhibit varying degrees of intimacy. The capacity for communication, vulnerability, and the touching communication of human sexual experiences is largely determined by the quality of maleness and femaleness achieved in the adolescent identity crisis. One overarching characteristic of intimacy in this sixth stage is the capacity for commitment in relationships.

The seventh stage (mid-life) is characterized by the conflict between generativity and stagnation. Mid-lifers either focus on the nurturance and care of others, or they erode in narcissistic self-fulfillment.[4]

The eighth stage (the senior years) is characterized by the conflict between integrity and despair. The older adult looks back and either feels

---

[2] Erikson's "adolescence" is having an earlier and earlier onset as we move into the twenty-first century. Many intermediate grade children already experience the conflict between identity and identity confusion. On the other hand, an identity "crisis" is often experienced later by some young adults, mid-life parents, and nonparental adults who have not yet resolved adolescent conflicts.

[3] Similarly, William James characterized adolescence as the paradigm of conversion and spiritual transformation. All the pieces of life are thrown into the air during adolescence, to be reconfigured in some future, undisclosed way. Adolescence, then, is analogous to the experience of spiritual conversion experienced throughout the life cycle.

[4] Feminist critics have suggested that locating the quest for generativity in mid-life is a male-skewed opinion. Women, they maintain, have been generative for years previous to mid-life. Carl Jung and others have written on mid-life as the dawning of a spiritual journey as a person enters the second half of life.

that life was worthwhile (integrity) or that life was filled with disappointment and cynicism (despair).[5]

Although Erikson's epigenetic theory has received criticism and additional nuances, its core truth continues to be evident. The eight stages still represent, with some existential authority, what it feels like to develop as a human being in Western society. What remains hidden in Erikson's theory are the substages contained within the central adolescent conflict between identity and identity confusion. Within the stage of adolescence, Erikson identified seven additional subconflicts. These conflicts are as follows:

1. Temporal perspective v. time confusion. Adolescents either develop some sort of handle on their future, or they are paralyzed by it. They stare at the future only with gloom. Many world realities—such as the nuclear build-up or the dismal economic prospect that the young will never know the prosperity of their parents—are examples of conditions that spark this confusion about the future in adolescents.

2. Self-certainty v. self-consciousness. Most of us can remember the awful bounce we experienced as teens between having a sense of bravado, or self-confidence, and having a restricting sense of self-depreciation. Adolescence is a time of struggle toward more consistent feelings of self-certainty.

3. Role experimentation v. role fixation. I agree with Erikson that the adolescent years ought to be a time of freedom in which teens are encouraged to experiment. The teen who rigidly locks into being a "straight-A student," a "superathlete," or a "dropout/burnout" is headed toward a life of conflict and stress.

4. Apprenticeship v. work paralysis. This subconflict involves the freedom to try a number of possible vocational pursuits. In opposition to this freedom is the feeling of being "stuck," or paralyzed, in one vocational direction—never experimenting/apprenticing with one's gifts or charisms.

5. Sexual polarization v. bisexual confusion. During this subconflict, sharp distinctions between male and female identities can become blurred, or one never develops good feelings about being a male or a female. A male

---

[5] Since Erikson wrote, gerontology has become a rapidly growing field for research and activity. Gerontologists now divide the senior years into many subcategories.

adolescent needs to develop a good feeling about his unique expression of maleness. Similarly, a female adolescent needs to develop healthy feelings about her unique expression of femaleness.

6. Leader followship v. authority confusion. According to Sharon Parks, young people need to have leaders or mentors; they cannot help but give their hearts to someone or to some cause. In this subconflict, the young person either develops a healthy approach to authority or becomes confused, thus following nonproductive and unsatisfying sources of authority.

7. Ideological commitment v. confusion of values. Adolescents, with their expanding intellectual and imaginative capacity, have commitment energy to give away. They willingly "lay down the nickel" for worthy causes congruent with the Christian understanding of God's Reign. Or they become lost in a sea of confusing spiritualities or value systems that cry out for their attention.

Along with these subconflicts, teens gradually acquire full physical sexual maturity. Although their bodies are adult, teens often have the emotional, social, and relational skills of children. Thus, adolescents tend to experiment sexually, vocationally, relationally, and individually. They re-evaluate the values they never questioned before. They gradually learn to make decisions and to live with the consequences.

Adolescence is an opportune time to learn shared decision making and democratic living in the classroom, family, and society. As the young person apprentices in various part-time work areas, he or she begins to assume an adult kind of accountability. Gradually, after experimentation with separation from his or her parents and family of origin, the older adolescent tends to grow in interdependence and, gradually, reenters family life.

Types of Adolescent Growth

Adolescents seem to grow in at least three different ways—continuously, surgently, and tumultuously. Continuous growth characterizes the patterns of young persons in a rather stable family environment, where family members have relatively stable personalities. These teens journey through the adolescent years with few traumatic episodes. Surgent growth, on the other hand, is somewhat chaotic. A teen in surgent growth tends to vacillate between periods of dormancy (apparent nongrowth) and spurts of obvious, accelerated growth. Tumultuous growth, however, is characterized by an unstable social context—a dysfunctional family with members who have unstable personalities and ego strengths. Tumultuous growth has been described by clinical psychotherapists as "growing up in a storm."[6]

The nature of adolescent growth—whether it is continuous, surgent, tumultuous, or a hybrid of two or three types—is largely influenced by parenting style. For the sake of simplicity, I will categorize parenting styles in three ways: the autocratic parent, the permissive parent, and the democratic parent. The autocratic parent wields power. He or she "lays down the law" and does not permit a home environment in which young people can develop their own views and opinions. The permissive parent lets teenagers do whatever they want. The young person is given full reign to act on impulse. The democratic parent, on the other hand, takes on the role of teacher. In attempting to teach family democracy, the parent upholds an environment that respects the rights of all family members. In addition to being a teacher, the parent guarantees mutual respect by invoking appropriate behavioral discipline.

In addition to parenting style, the adolescent's own personal lifestyle influences his or her pattern of growth. "Lifestyle" is a notion developed by Alfred Adler and further developed later by Rudolf Dreikers and Harold Mosak. "Lifestyle" refers to the unique vision and direction that one's life assumes. According to the Adlerian school of psychotherapy, each person's lifestyle is teleological, or purposeful. We put together a lifestyle unconsciously and nonverbally, from the unreflected-upon and unarticulated goals of achieving love and belonging.

Each person's lifestyle contains the following dynamics: self-concept, outlook on relationships, worldview, moral imperatives, and ideals. *Self-concept* refers to what we feel and think about ourselves. Unfortunately, our self-concept can get battered, distorted, and mistake-filled through the influence of our family of origin. Our *outlook on relationships* determines

---

[6] It seems that more and more children and adolescents in Western society are experiencing this last type of growth. Consequently, youth ministers need to find ways to provide young people with healthy experiences of family living and positive experiences of domestic Church.

what we expect from others and how we approach them. Our outlook can be healthy and accurate, or it can be filled with mistakes and learned misperceptions. Our *worldview* consists of our outlook on life in general. Whether we will be anxious, depressed, optimistic, or hopeful is largely determined by our view of life. *Moral imperatives* refers to the moral guidelines and compelling values that guide our relationships and conduct. *Ideals* are the vocational, relational, and interpersonal strivings and dreams that fire us up. They motivate us to act in certain ways and to keep on trying.

Adlerian psychologists describe personality theory in terms of an educational model. Except in the cases of severe psychosis, biochemical disorders, and addictions, most ordinary people simply "learn wrong," or develop mistaken notions in their self-concept, outlook on relationships, worldview, moral imperatives, and ideals. Through a process of reeducation, or therapy, most people can "unlearn" their notions and learn healthier new ones.

As I mentioned earlier, adolescence is classically described as the time for identity achievement. Traditional adolescent psychotherapy has spoken of three possible blocks to identity achievement: identity foreclosure, identity diffusion, and moratorium. In *identity foreclosure,* the parents or family—rather than the adolescent—choose the adolescent's life goals. In *identity diffusion,* the adolescent is propelled in many different directions, without a solid, integrating sense of self. In *moratorium,* the young person consciously or unconsciously declares a "time out" from the five life tasks and the challenge of choosing a lifestyle. This time out may be triggered by turbulence or crisis in another part of the teen's cultural landscape. Recent years have witnessed an apparently longer time needed by adolescents to achieve some sense of identity. Some young people seem to still be working on it in the mid or late twenties.

A New View of Young Adulthood

Describing the substages of adolescence does not adequately describe the experiences of all young people. An early mistake that I made in young adult ministry was to use the term "young adult" to describe everyone from eighteen to forty. Now I realize there are at least five subpopulations in the category of young adulthood.

The 18-22 group.[7] This age group consists both of young adults who go away to college and young adults who stay at home. The latter group of young adults may work or go to commuter college, or both. Some young people in this age group begin marriages; others remain single. During this stage, young adult developmental and spiritual issues—such as intimacy, sexuality, career, one's adult "dream," mentoring and being mentored, and the quest for meaning—emerge. At the same time, issues of adolescence may still be unresolved. Both the young adult issues and the unresolved adolescent issues accompany the young adult into all other phases of adulthood.

The 22-26 group. This age group is characterized by apprenticing in a career or a vocation, adult commitments, and adult relationships. Much of the literature on adult development says that the role of mentors is crucial at this stage of young adulthood. Young adults get a better sense of who they want to be by associating with people they respect—people whose inner life and abilities seem attractive.

The 26-32 group. In this age group, people solidify the essential adult life structure. Although these adults are still young, they are not "the new kids on the block." More and more responsibility is expected of them at this stage. Throughout both the 22-26 stage and the 26-32 stage, young adults marry, enter religious life, or choose to remain single. Human sexuality and sexual morality become significant concerns as young people confront the issue of intimacy and not just genital sexual experiences.

The 32-35 group. This stage can be quite turbulent. Often it involves a critical reevaluation of the initial life structure, including both career and relational commitments. Career change, divorce, and other major life shifts frequently occur in these years, which are but a tremor of the coming mid-life crisis. Companions and genuine communities can greatly assist the young person who is undergoing this transition.

The 35-40 group. This age group is characterized by a settling down, which some developmentalists have described as a "settling for the limitations of one's life situation." No one can stay in conflict indefinitely. Thus, young

---

[7] The numerical ages listed for the young adult stages are somewhat arbitrary in terms of when a stage begins or ends.

adults in this stage settle down or "settle for less" in preparation for the transition to mid-life.

In all of these substages, gender issues are constantly influencing the tapestry of young adulthood. Another influence, as we have seen in the early 1990s, is the economy. Economic issues seriously affect a young adult's approach to career, commitment, and relationships.

Historical Context

Thus ends our brief look at the classic understanding of the dynamics of youth. But are young people of different times in history really the same? What influence does historical context have on who we are? As James DiGiacomo indicates in his book *We Were Never Their Age,* today's young people are having experiences that youths of previous decades never had. Do these experiences give contemporary young people unique characteristics from those of earlier times? We'll explore this question in the next chapter.

2

The Characteristics of Contemporary Youth

T he 1980s and 1990s ushered in a new age: the era of the stressed child. In his two studies, *The Hurried Child* and *All Grown Up and No Place to Go,* David Elkind made popular the image of children without markers—adults who facilitate, or point to, a direction in life. Elkind lamented the number of parents who leave their children "psychological orphans." Instead of directing their children, these self-actualizing parents work at their own adolescence, which is chronologically delayed.[1]

Merton Strommen, in *The Five Cries of Youth,* further develops our emerging picture of contemporary youth. Strommen says he has heard "primal cries" coming from today's teens. One such cry is self-hatred, a lack of healthy completion of self-esteem and identity tasks. Another cry is that of the "psychological orphan." According to Strommen, even in two-parent families, many children and teens feel that they are orphaned, without significant mentors or guiding figures. A third cry of youth is social protest, disagreement with and rage toward the status quo of the world and society handed to them by parents and other adults. Insightfully, Strommen includes yet another cry—that of prejudice. Adolescents, in his words, can have remarkably closed

---

[1] When asked by a ministerial journal what a parish could better do to help stressed children, Elkind replied that the most urgent ministry may be to parents—to encourage them and train them to become markers for their children.

minds that leave them tremendously resistant to changed behavior. Finally, another cry of teens is that of joy. Despite the pain implicit in the previous cries, most teens retain the childlike tendency toward play.[2]

Stephen Schectman echoed Elkind and Strommen in his important study, *The Missing Link*. The "missing link" in contemporary life, Schectman feels, is quality time between parents/guardians and children. Schectman cautions American parents about "farming out" family functions, especially those functions calling for times spent together.

The U.S. bishops have popularized the same concern under the umbrella of "family consciousness." Family consciousness is an attempt to plan and evaluate pastoral ministry through the lens of "social context"—the network of a person's primary relationships. In the documents "A Family Perspective in Church" and "Society and Putting Children and Families First," the bishops warn against the individualism that characterizes most ministry. Ministers focus on individuals and not on the relational systems of which they are a part. Specific to youth ministry efforts, we too often have segregated youths away from their parents and families, and have focused on THEM. But, inevitably, the teens have to go back home, a reality often untouched by the Church's efforts.

As Bishop Michael Pfeifer said recently in a pastoral to the people of San Angelo, Texas, "If the Reign of God is to be experienced first and foremost, it must be in the family—in the simple yet important relational exchanges between family members." In fact, the rest of our educational and formational ministries become ineffective if we are not fostering God's Reign among family members. Such focusing on and ministry to the family is especially important during the adolescent period.

The Influence of Culture

Allan Bloom, in *The Closing of the American Mind,* deplores the culture we live in. As he sees it, we Westerners are increasingly nonreflective, nondiscerning, and reluctant to read, think, or meditate. In his follow-up

---

[2] I believe that Strommen's cries point to the ministry that adolescents need: listening, skill development in discernment, and preevangelization experiences that provide a firsthand taste of healthy intergenerational relationships.

work, *Giants and Dwarfs,* Bloom castigates the entire American system of public education. He sees it as ineffective because it is wedded to curriculum demands. Such an approach to education, Bloom contends, actually aborts genuine learning and the acquisition of wisdom. Instead, he suggests a "discipleship model," in which students learn by appropriating in some way the inner life of their teacher(s).

Another book, *Children at Risk: The Battle for the Health and Minds of Our Kids,* also focuses on the effects of the culture, or context, in which teenagers live. Coauthors Dr. James Dobson and Gary Bauer begin with the reality of abortion as a sinful toxin in present-day society. They believe that today's society is just as dangerous to young minds and souls as abortion is to a fetus. Dobson and Bauer highlight pornographic rock music and sexploitation media events as indicators of the abortive culture in which we live.[3] They describe young people's experience as being caught in the midst of a second "American Civil War." The antagonists in this war are gospel values and the values of our consumer society. As Dobson and Bauer see it, young people need to be introduced, as early as possible, to a personal relationship with Jesus Christ that leads them to a lifestyle of morality and integrity.

The October 8, 1990, edition of *Time* magazine contained the lead article, "Do We Care About Our Kids? America's Most Disadvantaged Minority." According to the research cited in this article, American teens are experiencing an extraordinary increase in violence, drug use, sexual activity, emotional problems, and alienation from parents and authority figures. *People* magazine (November 5, 1990), in an article entitled "Teens and Sex," similarly reported heightened sexual activity among teens. The article claimed that, despite the AIDS risk, seven out of ten American teens are sexually active.[4]

After these articles appeared, Ann Landers ran several "grass-roots" columns on the topic of sexual activity among teens. She received approximately 20,000 letters from concerned parents. One shift, Landers noted, was

---

[3] In her recent study, *Why Our Children Don't Think,* Dr. June Healy expresses a related concern over young people's preoccupation with media and computerized games.

[4] In the late eighties, Robert Coles and Geoffrey Stoks wrote *Sex and the American Teenager,* in which they also discussed the high prevalence of sexual activity among adolescents.

that teenage girls were initiating sexual activity just as often as the boys were. This contradicted the cultural stereotype that males are the aggressors of sex and that females respond.

All research—both on the academic and the grass-roots levels—reveals that the AIDS crisis has not slowed down sexual activity among teens. Instead, sexual experimentation seems to be beginning at an increasingly earlier age. Full sexual activity is now reported among twelve-, thirteen-, and fourteen-year-olds. One psychologist recently told me that American males typically have twenty sexual partners by age twenty. Females typically have seven partners. These sexually active young people seem to be suffering from loneliness, poor self-image, and poor mentoring from parents and guidance figures. The psychologist lamented that HIV-infected heterosexual youth could be the next epidemic in America.

More currently, the lead article in the August 10, 1992, issue of *Fortune* magazine was "Children in Crisis: The Struggle to Save America's Kids." Young people from Albuquerque, New York City, and Kansas City were interviewed about their views on and experiences of violence, crime, drugs, the dysfunctional side of American schools and family life, and absentee parent/guardians. Other articles in the same issue focused on epidemics (such as divorce, remarriage, illegitimacy, and gang membership) that have had a dramatic impact on altering the lives of young people. Most criticized were parents who give things—rather than time—to their kids. A second major criticism was directed at school systems that do little to prepare young people for the realities of work.

Indeed, today's young people nonreflectively breathe in the images of our consumer culture. Just as air pollution slowly damages lungs, so do the toxins of our dominant culture damage the minds, souls, and hearts of the young. Just consider some of these images of our culture: sexuality as mechanics, the reluctance to make commitments, the accumulation of possessions, hedonistic impulsiveness, fierce independence, addiction, and a morbid attitude toward struggle, pain, suffering, and death. These and other popular images stand in sharp contrast to the values and attitudes of Jesus.

Dr. Robert Coles, who has done extensive research on the spirituality and morality of children, recently wrote a book entitled *The Spiritual Life of Children.* In this book, Coles maintains that little children are, by nature, spiritual. This natural spirituality is evidenced in the spontaneous wondering and questions of the young child. By the time of later childhood and most certainly by adolescence, however, natural spiritual drives and curiosity are all but extinguished. This extinguishing is effected by cultural influences and adults in particular.

Although we cannot expect teenagers to run away from the world, I believe that today's youth ministers must give young people the needed skills to critique the dominant culture. As Pope Paul VI pointed out in his apostolic exhortation *Evangelii Nuntiandi,* the essence of evangelization lies in this: "I've got Good News for you; the Reign of God is here. Change your lives." (Mark 1:15) If God's Reign was the mission of Jesus, it also is ours. We must make serious attempts to understand, usher in, and facilitate this Reign of God within young people.

How are we to do this? What strategies should we follow in order to revive flickering faith in adolescents and young adults? The answer to these questions will be explored in the next chapter, which deals with youth evangelization.

3

What Is Youth Evangelization?

In a previous work, *Re-Imagining the Parish,* I emphasized imagination as the source for the images that determine our identity, our interfacing with culture, and our vision of the Church. Imagination is also at the heart of youth evangelization. Effective youth evangelization repatterns human imagination with the dominant images of the Reign of God.

The goal of evangelizing youth is to repattern the dominant images of self, culture, and Church in the minds of young people so that they can experience conversion. This conversion means several things. First, young people come to know their religious tradition (intellectual faith). Second, young people develop an I-Thou bond with God (relational faith). Third, young people put their faith into action, experiencing it especially in school and in the marketplace (performative faith). And fourth, young people embrace images and values that are more gospel-oriented (imaginative faith). In short, effective youth evangelization utilizes all the various dimensions of imagination highlighted by Maria Harris in *Teaching and Religious Imagination:* the contemplative (or confronting) imagination, the distancing (or ascetic) imagination, the compositive (or creative) imagination, and the archetypal (or sacramental) imagination.

As I have discussed in other books and articles, evangelization has both very precise and also very broad connotations. In its precise connotation, evangelization is an initial awakening of faith. Evangelization invites people to a relationship of love with God. This invitation has to be accompanied by related preevangelization techniques and skills. Such techniques and skills involve relational bonding with the people who are being evangelized. The minister must show sensitivity to the brokenness of those ministered to. He or she must take time to answer basic questions and respond to foundational life-search issues. Catechesis (faith seeking understanding) picks up on the spadework of evangelization. In some cases, theology builds on catechesis by systematizing and organizing the intellectual (cerebral) components of faith.

The broader connotation of evangelization involves understanding it from a "convergence" viewpoint. According to this viewpoint, the many diverse parish ministries all converge in one mission: evangelization. Evangelization means inviting people to God's Reign—to conversion, to discipleship, and to apostleship. This mission requires many efforts, many different types of ministries.

Mission is a crucial concept in the evangelization of youth. Mission, however, is not the same as maintenance. Maintenance parishes or institutions are concerned with tried-and-true structures and with regular attendees or participants. A maintenance Church is self-contained, closed in upon itself. On the other hand, a mission-oriented Church is concerned with those not yet attending—the inactive and the unchurched. Mission-oriented parishes try to engage as many people as possible in evangelization, rather than save this "job" for clerics or religious "professionals." Evangelizers who are aware of the many sides of the mission ahead of them, realize the need for multiple ministers and ministries. They realize that, in order to touch the number of youths needing evangelization, many diverse people (catechists, liturgists, spiritual directors, social ministers, etc.) have to be involved.

The broader connotation of youth evangelization demands a change in our language. It is no longer adequate to speak of the "youth minister." Rather, someone being hired for parish or pastoral youth work would be more accurately called the "coordinator," or the "animator" of youth ministries. To be a "youth minister" in the conventional sense is to engage too much in old-style, maintenance-minded, direct-delivery ministry. The youth minister spends too much time in direct service to a very few. No doubt, the services are often quite good. But this direct approach neglects the larger number of youths that populate the mission field. To be a "coordinator" of youth ministries means (in a sense) to clone oneself so that more and more young people receive adequate pastoring.[1]

Two words regarding both the precise and the broader connotations of evangelization are becoming important to me. These words are *spirituality* and *structures*.

Spirituality. Rollo May, in his recent study *The Cry for Myth,* speaks of the universal human need for meaning and stories—for myths that help to convey life's meaning. The pursuit of meaning is, at least in part, what spirituality is about. Young people, especially, are disinterested in the latest "churchified" programs, expectations, or obligations. Nevertheless, they do have a genuine spirituality, as exemplified in their search for meaning. I believe that youth evangelizers must focus specifically on "pastoring" the young, guiding them toward a heartfelt Christian spirituality and related sense of life's meaning.

Structures. To address young people's need for meaning requires that we devise innovative structures that work. Too often in evangelization work, we fail to clarify for ourselves the nature of the evangelical mission: to help young people find authentic Christian spirituality and meaning. Too often, also, we have inadequate, outmoded structures. The great challenge in pastoral planning is first to devise structures that fit the mission. A poorly defined mission and nonreflected-upon or unevaluated structures will result in busywork/maintenance youth ministry.

At the present time, Catholic youth evangelization structures often compartmentalize the various components of youth ministry to the point of ineffectiveness. There is a great unevenness in the "product." For example, one parish may have a youth social program. Another parish may sponsor a catechetical program for adolescents. A third parish may provide its young people with a retreat program. Few parishes, however, get the various pieces in a teleological flow, thus calling young people to discipleship and vocation.

---

[1] I believe the reason there is such a big turnover in youth ministers is that high "mission" expectations are placed on them, but—because of a "maintenance" direct-delivery model—they are able to touch only a few members of the target youth audience.

Perhaps we can learn from the interdenominational evangelical world that each parish doing youth ministry is no longer possible or even desirable. Maybe our results would be better if parishes pooled their resources—both in terms of finances and personnel—to reach out to young people in an expanded sort of way. Perhaps what we need are holistic youth centers sponsored by a number of parishes—with staffs adequate both for the scope of the evangelical mission and the large target population of preteens, teens, and young adults.

In the interdenominational evangelical world, structures are planned, evaluated, and reshaped according to the mission. Because the goal of evangelizing ministry is to facilitate the holistic conversion of our young people, parishes and pastoral institutions need to take a long, hard look at whether or not their current structures are facilitating that conversion.

The Characteristics of Conversion

What are the characteristics of conversion? First of all, conversion involves a felt experience of being in "dislocation," that is, of being "at sea," of being in "dis-ease." All of the great conversion stories in Scripture involve the motif of being on a journey, of being dislocated. The pain of being "a dislocated self" is an indication that conversion is possibly taking place.

Dislocation is part of the landscape of moving from childhood through adolescence. Indeed, the dislocation of adolescence (which was discussed in the previous chapter) can be the beginning of a breaking apart that becomes a breakthrough to authentic gospel living. Adolescent dislocation, however, can also be a cause for breakdown, alienation, and deterioration. In order for adolescent dislocation to move toward positive resolution, young people need trained mentors and pastoring figures to nurture them and give them witness, both verbally and behaviorally.

Another characteristic of conversion is the assumption of a critical, reflective attitude toward the world and the dominant culture. One of the best things we can do for young people is to aid them in developing the skills of critical reflection. As we have already discussed, young people can be "negatively evangelized" in the values of consumer-oriented, middle-class America. The process of negative evangelization is subtle, often insidious, as young people unconsciously and nonreflectively swallow the images flashed at them by the media. Critical reflection, on the other hand, involves a sharpening awareness of the values and images implicit in advertising and entertainment. The young person learns to evaluate the cultural images in terms of the respect for human life and creation that is present or missing in them. The young person develops a growing awareness of values and images that are endorsed by the preaching and ministry of Jesus.

A good example of critical reflection can be found in Don Kimball's techniques and strategies for evaluating the appropriateness of a rock song. Kimball stresses that adults who tell young people to stay away from the values of the media are, in the long run, ineffective. Instead, young people need to be taught a new kind of inculturation. They need to evaluate the dominant culture in terms of its congruence or incongruence with the Gospel. Young people especially need to become aware of those cultural messages that degrade the person or human sexuality or any subgrouping of the human family. They also need to become aware of those messages that glorify violence and aggression.

Steps in the Conversion Process

Maryknoll missionary Father John Walsh, working with Jesuit Father James DiGiacomo, identified a number of steps that indicate the evangelization-conversion process is taking place in a person's life. Some of these steps have special significance for our discussion of youth evangelization.

After working with Japanese young people who were converting from Eastern religions to Christianity, Walsh noticed in them the presence of a "coefficient of anxiety." The young converts were doing more than changing denominations. Rather, in embracing Catholicism, the young people were very consciously giving up something in order to take on something new. Walsh further reflected that this "coefficient of anxiety" was missing in most religious education programs in America. As Walsh saw it, people in U.S. religious education and sacramental programs seemed to approach the programmatic steps and stages as a head trip, a solely intellectual endeavor. These people were not engaging in true conversion—the change of heart and behavior. If we were to apply Walsh's findings to youth evangelization, then it would seem that adolescent/young adult conversion ought to include an amount of anxiety or giving up something.

Walsh also identified two other steps in the evangelization-conversion process that are applicable to youth ministry. First, in the process of evangelization-conversion, the person must somehow experience the "primal cry for more." This experience brings the person face-to-face with his or her need for the transcendent, the need for God. Second, the person must also experience a "primal cry for help," the realization that he or she cannot get through life alone. Similar to the first primal cry, this one is an awareness of the person's incompleteness and of the consequent need for relationships, for community.

I believe that the felt need for God and the felt need for community are two necessities in the evangelization-conversion process of young people. Because many young people are not in touch with their deepest needs, youth evangelization must penetrate young people's hearts and imaginations to help them become aware of their spiritual needs and, thus, become open to true conversion. Effective youth evangelization means effective marketing of Jesus and the Reign of God. The goal of evangelical marketing is the same as marketing in business: to change negative perceptions into curiosity, interest, want, need, and action.

Conversion and Imagination

True conversion repatterns the imagination. Many young people today operate out of dominant images that are either poorly informed (the result of mistaken learning) or dysfunctional (they do not result in a sense of meaning or belonging). Such mistaken or dysfunctional images produce misconceptions regarding God (who is seen as distant and punishing) and Church (which is regarded as hierarchical and boring).

In the April 14, 1990, issue of *America* magazine, William O'Malley (a Jesuit teacher and longtime youth minister) warned about the prevalence of "placebo Christianity" among our young people. With both a tongue-in-cheek style and a cutting accuracy, O'Malley described the "creed" of the apparently religious adolescent:

I sort of believe in God, who . . . lives somewhere out there . . . impossible to communicate with. . . . I sort of believe in Jesus Christ, who preached that we ought to be nice and help . . . our friends. I believe in the Holy Spirit, which is just a different name for . . . love. . . . I don't honestly believe in the Roman Catholic Church; Christian is better. . . . The real Church is . . . a fuzzy fellowship . . . [with] good feelings. . . . I believe God forgives our sins . . . even when we don't have the time . . . to ask for it. . . . And I believe in the resurrection of the dead, . . . but that is a long, long way off. Amen.

Many young people today believe that the mission of Jesus was (and is) to make people "nice." But Jesus calls us to embrace culturally alternative dominant images that lead to a change—a truly evangelized lifestyle. This lifestyle will often result in division, rather than in nice, tepid friendliness.

Margaret O'Brien Steinfels, editor of *Commonweal* magazine, approached the issue of poorly evangelized young people in an address to CORPUS (Corps of Reserve Priests United for Service) on June 22, 1991, in New York City. Steinfels said:

Is there anyone who is confident that the Faith has been successfully passed on to the next generation? . . . that the post-conciliar period has produced a religious renewal among young people? We await the return of the baby boomers (to the Church). . . . But . . . the greater number . . . are passing into adulthood and career with a very meager store of Catholicism's theological and spiritual riches. . . . They often lack the most elementary habits of prayer or understanding of the sacraments.

In a true conversion experience, the imagination jumps from inadequate cultural images to the dominant images of the Reign of God. Such imaginative jumps, facilitated by evangelizing ministry, need two supportive entities: *confirmation* that God is indeed present and communicating in human experience, and an *environment* that nurtures and fosters the conversion process. Confirmation is provided by other human beings who have had similar interior experiences. These people are one's community or faith community. The environment that best nurtures the conversion process is worship or liturgy.

As stated previously, the evangelization-conversion process flows from preevangelization, which involves relational bonding. Preevangelization with young people requires a great deal of patience in dealing with their mistaken or dysfunctional beliefs, especially regarding God and the Church. Evangelization shapes the imagination and beliefs of young people; effective evangelization leads to conversion. Conversion, in turn, flows into catechesis, the subject of the next chapter.

4

Youth Catechesis

S ome years ago, Michael Warren wrote that adolescent catechesis had become so weak that it was, in fact, "dead." Warren charted the course of catechetical history in the United States with three words: *contact, content,* and *communion.* During the first era of youth ministry, what mattered was contact with young people, largely through athletic and social activities. The second era was concerned with content—a schooling model of transmitting religious information to adolescents. The new era facing us today is the communion period. The communion model of youth ministry still values contact and content, but emphasizes the relational. According to this model, the gospel message is best incarnated in loving, communal experiences. Communion with others is a taste of what it is like to be in communion with the Holy One. Warren felt that the contact and content models were inadequate; instead, he advocated an integrated view in which contact and content lead to multidimensional communion.

A similar discussion using different language has taken place recently among religious educators. These educators talk about the inadequacy of the "schooling model" of religious education, both in the format of parochial school religious education and parish religious education programs. One reason the schooling model is inadequate is that it is anchored to the academic school calendar. The typical location of the educational events and programs is a classroom. A textbook with a predetermined scope and sequence is the main learning tool. Parents are minimally involved; the person bearing the biggest burden of responsibility is the catechist or teacher. The goal of the school model is transmission/assimilation of information ABOUT God and Church. While young people learn prayers, they are rarely taught to pray. Scripture study and usage is at a minimum, only to the degree that it supports the scope and sequence of the textbook. Likewise, the school model underplays the importance of active membership in a eucharistic assembly and community. Sacraments are presented as "holy things" that young people prepare for, receive, and then forget as they get on with real life.

In contrast to the schooling model is the "initiation model" of religious education. The goal of the initiation model is the gradual incorporation of a young person (and his or her family) into the eucharistic community. The initiation model follows the liturgical year; thus catechetical opportunities can take place fifty-two weeks a year. The Eucharist is central to the model, with sessions often connected in some way to the celebration of Mass. Parents and guardians are involved in the process, with the catechist taking on the supportive role of helping parents accomplish their mission as religious educators.

In the initiation model, Scripture is central. The lectionary becomes the "textbook" of religious education. Preparing for sacraments is never viewed as preparing for the reception of "holy things." Rather, sacramental catechesis is preparation for a way of living. Conversion is seen as a holistic experience, effecting a change of mind, heart, and behavior. Young people not only learn prayers, but, in fact, learn to pray. Real apprenticing in service and ministry replaces token service projects. The essence of the catechumenate experience is something that all parishioners—not just the catechumens and candidates—experience. Young people no longer drop in and out of catechesis, based on their desire for receiving sacraments; nor do they "graduate" from catechesis after the eighth grade. Instead, initiation catechesis becomes a lifelong journey into discipleship.

I think we need to look more deeply into what we intend to do when we engage in catechesis with youth. Thomas Groome, in *Christian Religious Education,* highlights the ideal components, or elements, in the process of catechesis. He contends that religious education has to be political in nature; it has to lead to a certain kind of behavior or activity. Groome also says that religious education must pay attention to the activity of God present in human experience. This is what Jesus meant by the Reign of God, the active presence of God in time. Religious education shares this vision of the Reign of God and echoes the story of the Christian community (the tradition of the Church).

As Groome sees it, the purpose of catechesis is to foster a faith that is rooted in belief, trust, and doing. The process of catechesis ought to lead participants to greater freedom. Ideally, catechesis ought to impart the skills of theological reflection—the ability to compare human experience with what the culture says and what Scripture and Church tradition say. Hopefully, the result will be a response that is filled with gospel values and vision.

Let us consider some additional principles regarding youth catechesis, keeping in mind the values of the initiation model.

- Catechesis is oriented toward lifelong conversion. All structures and planning need to keep this goal in mind.
- Catechesis ought to incorporate the *experience* of Church. Catechesis must not just talk about, but must actually provide, experiences of communion.
- Catechesis must "speak the language of the age," employing contemporary media resources. Critical reflection is a skill shared in catechesis, especially regarding dominant culture.
- Catechesis is best done in the context of community. Catechesis gives significant time to relationship-building between catechist and young person and between the peer members of the discipleship community.
- Catechesis is a pursuit of gospel truth. It is "awakened faith" (pre-evangelization and evangelization) seeking understanding. To be truly effective, catechesis employs ritual and liturgical experiences; it touches not just the intellect but also one's heart and imagination.
- Catechesis with adolescents necessitates the use of both andragogical and pedagogical skills—that is, skills for adult- and child-centered learning.
- Those doing youth catechesis should have discerned gifts for this ministry.
- Catechesis often has great impact if it addresses the genuine questions and life searches of young people. To do this best, catechesis must be

coordinated with a network of other ministers and ministries in order to effect holistic conversion in a young person. Catechetical ministry is truly collaborative.

The Challenge of Adolescent Catechesis

In 1986, the National Federation for Catholic Youth Ministry issued a foundational document entitled *The Challenge of Adolescent Catechesis: Maturing in Faith*. The document specifies goals and challenges for the catechesis of adolescents. According to this document, catechesis must lead young people to a personal relationship with, and experience of, Jesus Christ. In other words, the making of disciples should be one of the primary goals of adolescent catechesis. In order for catechesis to be effective, the *Challenge* document calls youth ministers to a better understanding of the adolescent as a developing human person.

Maturation rates differ among teens, and the *Challenge* document reminds catechists to respect these differences. Catechists need to use unique approaches with the younger adolescent (11-15). Similarly, catechists must give attention to the needs and developmental issues—especially the quest for freedom and autonomy—of the older adolescent (15-19). The *Challenge* document also calls for a growing sensitivity about recruiting and serving ethnic young people, better cooperation between parishes and parochial schools in developing adolescent catechetical programs, and the collaboration of various ministries to accomplish a comprehensive approach to youth ministry.

Furthermore, the *Challenge* document states that reoccurring themes— Jesus Christ, Scripture, Church, prayer, social action, lifestyle, and critical reflection—require constant, sensitive attention. The *Challenge* document also highlights specific roles that need to be actualized in order for adolescent catechesis to be effective. These roles include the advocate, the resource person, the coordinator, and the catechist.

- *The advocate.* This person educates parish leaders about the need for, the importance of, and the current directions of adolescent catechesis.
- *The resource person.* This person acts as a conduit to available resource material in adolescent catechesis.

- *The coordinator.* This person organizes the catechetical program with a planning team.
- *The catechist.* This person is responsible for direct delivery of the catechetical program to teens.

Although I am a presbyter, I have also had the role of youth minister (or, as we have redefined, "coordinator" of youth ministries) in three parishes. In my most successful effort, over three hundred young people were involved in catechesis. At St. Hubert's Parish in Hoffman Estates, Illinois, we had regular listening sessions that tried to tap into the subjective lens, or the spiritual wonderings, of the teens. Learning modules were then created around the teens' interests and needs. Built into every module was ample flexibility, so that the catechists could address subjective needs while also insuring the handing on of our faith tradition. To tap further into subjective needs, peer ministry was built into every catechetical session. Catechists were encouraged to keep "question or issue" boxes available so that the teens could readily drop in suggestions or questions for the peer ministry component.

As the structure progressed, every young person was encouraged to go on a teen retreat. Thus, we offered many opportunities for retreats throughout the year. One of the best overnight retreats that I have ever been a part of was one on human sexuality. The retreat format and the length of time spent with the teens allowed us to reflect together on various issues of sexuality. At the same time, I was able to present some of the wisdom of the Church on sexual questions.

In terms of the *Challenge* document, I very much assumed the roles of coordinator and resource person in my work in each of the three parishes. We did not use textbooks as such. Rather, every young person was given an empty folder with the title of the module on it. On a regular basis, the teens received articles that were pertinent to the subject matter. By the end of the learning module, each young person's folder was filled with articles. The young people were also encouraged to keep a journal of feelings, thoughts, and guided reflections in the same folder. In short, the teens assembled their own textbooks.

The major catechetical tools I used were a copy of the Scripture and the relevant folders for each module. As resource person, I worked directly with a coordinator of high school catechesis who, in turn, provided resources to the catechists. As the FLAME (Friendship, Leadership, Acceptance, Ministry, Education) model emerged, many people were in regular need of training and formation, just to be catechists. These people worked with other people in training who were preparing for various youth ministries (such as spiritual direction, social ministry, peer ministry, liturgy, etc.).

One catechetical resource I try to emphasize with catechists is the centrality of the creed. The creed is an articulation of the essentials of our faith. I try to help catechists see that the doctrine expressed in the creed is symbol/image talk, expressive of life-changing realities and experiences. Trinity, redemption, and resurrection were life-changing experiences before they were doctrinal pronouncements.[1] I also make available to catechists several copies of Richard McBrien's *Catholicism,* so that they can better understand the historical evolution of Catholic doctrine and tradition.

A Note about Older Teens and Young Adults

In general, initiation catechesis involves immersion into various strata of community: the large assembly, intergenerational and peer communities, and the family as domestic Church. Liturgy, the communal life, family involvement, breaking open the word of God, and handing on the tradition of the Church are key pieces of youth catechesis. It has been my experience that older teens and young adults need different types of learning formats than younger teens. As high school students move into junior and senior year and beyond, more informal gatherings—such as breakfasts and potluck dinners—have proven successful and effective. I will discuss at length these and other specific strategies I have used with older teens and young adults in chapter ten. Meanwhile, the next chapter will discuss one of the vehicles through which youth catechesis takes place—the intergenerational and peer-oriented community.

---

[1] In another book, *The Reconciling Parish,* I presented a model formation process based on the Creed, providing adults with an intuitive experience of the core realities of our faith. A helpful, intellectual resource in this area is *The Creed* (Twenty-Third Publications, 1987).

5

Intergenerational and Peer-Group Communities

A colleague of mine reacted with humor to a bumper sticker she had seen. The sticker read, "Subvert the dominant paradigm!" The presence of such words on a bumper sticker points out the popularity these days of talking about paradigms—our ways or models of doing things.

In Church circles, a great deal of attention has been given to paradigm shifts in how we "do Church" or "do ministry." The shifts have been variously described—from "programs" to "process," from "ministry of the ordained" to "ministry of the baptized," from "hierarchy" to "community." Many experts on parish life say that the Holy Spirit seems to be calling the Church to a more communal way of being Church and parish. The primary tool, or agent, of this new communal paradigm is the basic Christian community—small intentional communities, or small faith groups.

Small communities are not just another fad or another parochial buzzword. They are, in fact, a retrieval and renewal of an ancient way of being Church. In contrast to today's dominant culture of fierce privatism and independence, a prophetic ecclesiology permeates small communities. This ecclesiology states that we have been made for communion, for union, with each other and with God. Small communities are an experience of Church and also an experience of life in the image of God, who is communion as Trinity.

Small communities intentionally focus on the spiritual, but they also focus on reality. The Good News is always wedded to real issues in the world, in the news, in the neighborhood, in the dominant culture, in the here and now. There is a blending of the spiritual and the political. There is also a healthy emphasis on baptismal spirituality and on ministry rooted in the discernment of charisms. Thus, in a small community there are not some religion professionals who serve while the rest are recipients of service. Instead, all members of the community minister to one another.

Ministering community members do not operate out of a haphazard "volunteerism" model. Instead, their specific ministry flows from their unique giftedness, their share in the power of God and the Holy Spirit. For this reason, small communities devote significant time to discernment, to sifting through and identifying each person's giftedness. After each person discerns individually, the rest of the community is consulted for confirmation or challenge. Through this process, clericalism is resisted; there are no "special few." Rather, the small community becomes a gathering of equals, a gathering of servant leaders.

Characteristics of Small Communities

Many people in today's secular society regard spirituality as an escape from the real world. In contrast to this belief, members of small communities are trained to hold the Reign of God, the Church, and the world in healthy balance. Human needs, relational issues, even issues concerning business and the economy are very much the agenda of small Christian communities.

Small communities tend to go through stages of development or evolution. One way of charting such development is to note the transition stages from group to community. A gathering of people still in the group stage can get together for any one of a number of reasons—social, political, business, etc. The group is simply an assembly of people relating as people with each other. A group evolves into a community, however, when its focus on the real world takes on the additional dimensions of attending to the spiritual that is incarnate in the real, the ordinary. This is why Christian communities are occasionally called "intentional" communities. Community members consciously intend to pay attention to the faith dimension of their lives.

Community members share four essential activities with each other. First, the members pray with each other, and therefore need training in and the experience of shared prayer. Second, the members share Scripture with each other, and therefore need training in nonfundamentalist approaches to the Bible. Third, members share life with each other, and therefore need experiences in self-disclosure. Finally, community members minister to one another, to the larger community, and to the marketplace. In order to determine their individual charism for ministry, community members need various levels of discernment.

Young People and Small Communities

Usually, some common bond attracts people to a group that eventually becomes a community. As we begin to explore small communities as the healthiest environment for youth ministry, we need to ask ourselves who or what would bring young people to such a gathering in the first place. I believe the magnetic force that attracts young people to a group or community has little to do with God or Church. Rather, the more likely initial attraction is some sort of enjoyment or fun experience, and also some relationships or friendships that promise rewarding companionship. This preevangelization starting point can, and often will, develop into a more substantive motivation for membership; or the young people may stay at the level of "fun-seeking."

In my experience, small communities for youth evangelization are most effective when they are intergenerational in nature, when at least three age levels are interacting with each other—the adolescents, young adults, and either mid-lifers or senior citizens. Clearly, the role of the adult in these communities is to provide mentoring or guidance to those who are younger. But here also, the discernment of charisms must be emphasized. Some adults in the small group may be gifted for social ministry or fun events. Other adults may be equipped for the ministry of the Word, for evangelization, for catechesis, for faith witnessing, for Scripture sharing, or for leading discussions. Some adults may be gifted in liturgy and worship. Still others may be especially blessed with skills for pastoral care or guidance.[1] The role of the coordinator

---

[1] One adult in each community should be discerned to be the leader, or pastor, of the small community.

of youth ministries is to help the adults discern how they have been specifically gifted for youth ministry and also to provide these adults with the necessary training.

Peer Ministry

In these intergenerational small communities, peer-to-peer youth ministry should not be underestimated. In my experience, I have found it important—early in the process of generating a plan and process for youth ministry—to develop leadership and ministerial skills among the young people themselves. As much as possible, I have tried to foster the discernment of ministerial gifts among young people. A vehicle that I have found helpful in achieving this goal is a Youth Ministry Leadership Retreat-Vacation. After general reach-out and also some one-on-one encouragement and initiation, it has been my practice to take over one hundred adolescents on a four- or five-day seminar for training. The work sessions at the retreat-vacation are kept brief, and are carefully sandwiched between organized fun or social time and personal free time. At these work sessions, I give the potential youth leaders an overview of the ministries involved in a small community. Among the ministries I cover are the following:

- *Leadership.* Who is gifted to be the youth leader or co-leader of a small community?
- *Youth Ministry Board representatives.* Who feels gifted to represent the various intergenerational communities on the governing board that integrates all youth efforts, from junior high to young adulthood?
- *Retreat ministers.* Who is willing to serve on a committee that helps to plan all youth retreats?
- *Worship ministers.* Who wants to help plan youth-related worship activities?
- *Social ministers.* Who can research and help plan fun activities for the entire youth population and all youth communities?
- *Justice ministers.* Who can research areas of justice and then connect individuals and communities to various needs?
- *Fund-raisers.* Who will brainstorm and coordinate efforts to raise funds to help defray the costs of youth events?

- *Reach-out ministers.* Who feels called to bring new members into the youth communities?[2]

While these are standard ministries, other ministries materialize when there is need for them. The process, I admit, is sloppy, and there are the usual problems of trying to teach adolescents responsibility. Having several adults in each community is essential. These adults do the ministry for which they are gifted and also "mentor" young people in accomplishing their ministries. It is important for the adult ministers not to DO FOR the teens, but to be there to support the teens in their ministry. Involving all teenage members of the small communities in the process of ministry (according to gifts or charisms) and evangelization (reach-out) is also essential.

After giving the potential youth leaders an overview of these ministries, I also give them some experience in practicing the skills needed for such ministries. For example, on the retreat-vacation the teens learn to:
- run a meeting and participate in a meeting;
- do a mailing to advertise an upcoming youth event;
- work in a youth ministry office to do effective reach-out to other youths via the phone;
- speak publicly in church during the announcement time to appeal to young people; and
- witness to faith by giving brief talks about one's religious experience, either in a small community, or in a large assembly of small communities.

In addition to practicing these skills, every young person on the retreat-vacation is mentored in basic human-relations skills.[3] Young people genuinely seem to enjoy learning these skills and then using them—not only in their ministerial activities, but also in their interactions with friends and family.

---

[2] It has been my practice to create among the young people a healthy competition in reaching out to new members. I have also given each small community the rotating responsibility of working in the youth ministry office. Community members call all adolescents on the current list or send mailings to them—inviting them either to membership or to an upcoming event.

[3] Because the human-relations skills are available in an easily adaptable form from the work of Robert Carkhuff, Thomas Gordon, Gerald Egan, Michael Popkin, and others, we do not have to do an exhaustive training presentation.

What are these human-relations skills? The following list includes some examples.

- *Attending to others through body language.* Through various exercises, young people get in touch with their typical body language, and how—through discipline and practice—they can improve body posture to facilitate total communication. Crucial skills include eye contact and maintaining an "open" posture.

- *Active listening.* Using training techniques, we encourage young people to listen accurately to others for content (what happened). Then, through simple sentences, the young people mirror, reflect, or paraphrase back what they have heard.

- *Advanced active listening.* Teens are taught to "hear" feelings not directly expressed by a speaker, but nonetheless present in an encounter. Then the teens are trained to share with the speaker their perception of the speaker's feelings. The speaker, in turn, is free to agree or disagree with the teen's assessment.

- *Confrontation and "I feel" statements.* All human relations seem to include a certain amount of conflict and discord. This conflict and discord need not, however, deteriorate into deep alienation. Alienation happens if two people in conflict begin to put each other down with pejorative comments, which are usually led with the pronoun "you." ("You did this . . ." "You made me feel like . . .") Instead, teens are taught to respond to conflict with "I feel" statements. Such statements objectively describe the conflictual behavior or event and how it made the teen feel. ("I felt hurt when . . ." "I don't understand why . . .")

- *Win-win solutions to conflict.* In win-lose conflicts, one person wins and the other person loses. Of course, no one wants to lose. In win-win training, young people are taught "transformational relating." Antagonists learn how to transform their positions enough to create something new that is agreeable to both parties.

These skills may seem like a waste of time to the catechetical culture that often emphasizes content. I believe, however, that human-relations skills are especially important for young people to learn. Young people have the capacity to be impulsive, and therefore are too often unnecessarily cruel to each other in what they say. If, on the other hand, young people practice human-relations skills, they stand a chance to softening verbal harshness among peers and in familial settings. In addition to this "human" dimension, there is a deeper truth as well: These skills allow us to put into practice, to live out, the Reign of God. As Bishop Michael Pfeifer (San Angelo, Texas) has written in his already mentioned pastoral letter "The Family and the Kingdom of God," effective human-relations skills are young peoples' "first taste" of the Reign of God.

The setting for a retreat-vacation is usually a retreat house or camping site with multiple resources for summer recreation (swimming, horseback riding, competitive sports) as well as available space for worship (either outside or indoors). These days away can be remarkable opportunities for community building, small group formation, skills development, and simple experiences of spirituality and faith sharing.

The "Heart" of Youth Ministry

In the FLAME model of youth evangelization, there is a weekly COR night. *Cor* is Latin for "heart." The COR night is the heart of youth ministry. The most faithful small group leaders and members attend this meeting. The evening consists of three parts: business in each small community; fun or social experiences among the various communities; and a closing religious experience consisting of Scripture, drama, music, and witness talks done by adults and teens.

Each of the three parts of a COR evening is ministered by the young people themselves. The business components are chaired by the leader(s) of each small community. (The business consists of announcements and organizational issues around upcoming events for all young people in the area.) Each week, a different small community takes responsibility for planning and implementing the social component of the meeting. Each week, another small community takes responsibility for the religious experience. The entire evening is convened by the officers of the FLAME organization (president, vice president, treasurer, and secretary) who are chosen by a process of discernment in the communities.

I must admit that it can take years for a COR night to run effectively. In my first experience of implementing the process, it was five years before I could stand at the back of such a meeting and simply be present. By this time, the adult and youth ministers had been thoroughly trained and were executing their responsibilities.

The weekly COR night is only the initial step in the process of youth evangelization. Additional small community meetings are held for catechesis, spiritual direction, retreats, liturgical events, etc. The COR meeting is in a public place with a welcoming environment. Subsequent small community meetings are usually held in the homes of the participating adult ministers.

What If?

By now you may be asking what youth ministers should do if some teens do not want more than the COR night. Most likely, only some young people will stay in the same group for years, experiencing growth through evangelization, catechesis, spiritual direction, celebration, and follow-up formation. Most often, teens maintain their COR group as a hub, but gather in other groups for the more advanced steps of catechesis, discipleship, commitment, and ministry.[4] No prepackaged answers regarding these situations can be suggested in this book. I believe if we are committed to "organically growing" youth ministry communities, then the members themselves—in the local situation—must make adaptive decisions that apply to their situation. There are no right or wrong ways to structure the small groups. Rather, whatever works is what is important.

---

[4] This is the model at St. John Neumann Parish in St. Charles, Illinois.

—6—

The Process of Forming Disciples

I have no time for myself. . . . Everyone else sets the schedule for me. . . .
There isn't enough time in the day. . . . If only I had the chance, I'd sleep
all day. . . ." Are these comments from some mid-life executive on the verge
of burnout? No, they are comments from junior high and senior high students,
aired on a recent radio talk show in Chicago. The teenagers were reflecting
on the stress and busyness of their lives. In many ways, these young people
represent the growing number of children and adolescents who do not have
time to "be kids," because their parents set high standards for them and treat
them as "trophies" to display to others.

A recent study (0-3: the National Center for Clinical Infant Programs)
shows how millions of children are not properly being prepared for college
or for adult life. Young people today seem to be lacking in curiosity,
persistence, confidence, and a spirit of cooperation—qualities that used to
be acquired during the first three years of life. These foundational attitudes,
the study maintains, are more important than learning to read, write, or
count. The absence of these attributes—the failure to develop them—is due,
among other factors, to dysfunctional family living, poor family health care,
domestic violence, and substance abuse in the home.

Both the radio talk show and the national study about the toxicity of
young people's lives are evidence of the need to understand and minister to

youths in the context of their culture. As Sharon Parks points out in *The Critical Years,* most young people today are mentored by the ladder of ascendancy (or "the fat wallet")—a major image of our dominant culture. Our young people, echoes Father William O'Malley, learn their work ethics and approach to school from Ferris Buehler; they learn their sexual ethics from Madonna. The implications for youth ministry are apparent. Only after we become increasingly aware of the influence of culture on our young will we be able to discern what they most need from us. I would suggest that low on the priority list of youth ministry is the ability to mouth something from *Catechism of the Catholic Church.* While religious literacy is valuable, the ache of young lives today demands something more profound.

Some years back, an evangelical youth minister asked me this question: "Do you disciple your young people?" His question has stayed with me as a challenge. Do we disciple adolescents and young adults? "Of course," I defensively responded. But I knew, and I still know, that the Catholic Church does not disciple young people all that well. Catholic young people are largely estranged from the Church and are bored with what youth ministry has to offer.

Discipling Young People

Just what does the word *disciple* mean as a verb? To understand that, we must first take a look at the meaning of *disciple* as a noun. In ancient Jewish times, a disciple was a devotee, or an apprentice, to a rabbi. The goal of the rabbi-disciple relationship was not the appropriation of intellectual content, but an absorption of the inner life of the teacher. Discipling was, in essence, value sharing, the sharing of one's inner life. In youth ministry today, I believe we must disciple young people in the inner life of Jesus. At the core of discipling is the dimension of personal witness. Youth ministers must give evidence of their own transforming relationship with Christ and the Christian community. This means that youth ministers—whether they are mid-lifers or senior citizens—must have a great deal of inner work going on in them. They must be experiencing their own conversion-discipleship journey.

Hopefully, we youth ministers will disciple and mentor young people in the values of the Reign of God: love, peace, service, friendship, prayerfulness,

God-centeredness, honesty, and hope (conviction about the resurrection going on in our midst). In discipling young people, we must seek to give them a taste of this alternative lifestyle, or vision. Indeed, gospel living is countercultural, rubbing against the grain of mainline religion, society, and government.[1]

The motif of discipling is one of process, or journey. Adults who disciple young people need to be committed to long-term care; they need to be patient with the process. In a true spirit of preevangelization, we need to accept young people wherever they are at, showing respect even for the opinions and values we do not agree with.

The discipling process of preevangelization, evangelization, and catechesis is teleological and purposive. This full-cycle vision of youth ministry is not about "doing stuff" for kids. The goal of these various stages of religious education is the making of disciples. Young disciples are not people in flight from the world, but rather, people with feet firmly planted in the world, in reality. With the help of ministers, young people gradually discover alternative values to those offered by the dominant culture. Young people believe in and begin to live these values because they have seen them alive and present in the adults with whom they have interacted.

"Appropriating values" and "being in process" are two key elements of discipleship. There are others. For disciples, there is no graduation. Disciples will always be a flawed, vulnerable group, as were the first disciples of Jesus. But in that humanity, that imperfection, disciples continue to search for norms with which to live life fully. Their norm is the interior life, or vision, of Jesus.

Disciples Becoming Apostles

Ideally, disciples discover another side to their identity—apostleship. In the New Testament, the disciples were the students of Jesus; the apostles, however, were those who continued Jesus' mission to the world. Likewise, a contemporary apostle is not afraid to bring his or her faith to the marketplace—to school, neighborhood, or family. Apostles realize that faith

---

[1] A Dominican priest, Chuck Daum, says that people in ministry need to realize that most Americans have a preferential option for the middle class. This option deeply influences how much we allow Christ and God's Reign to influence our lives.

is incomplete without putting the Gospel into action and changing society with the power of one's witness.

As Chapter 1 mentioned, Erik Erikson described the adolescent years as a conflict between ideological commitment and value confusion. If we apply Erikson's description to modern-day youth ministry, then it seems to me that we often underwhelm our young people with insipid programming. Remember, teens and young adults have commitment energy to give away. They will give that energy either to the values of the dominant culture or to the values of the Reign of God.

Granted, the process of discipling young people and helping them become apostles is messy. This process does not fit neatly into an obsessive-compulsive's ministry programs. As leaders in youth ministry, we need to keep in perspective the vision of what we are about. If we have an energizing dream directing us, immediate successes or failures in ministry will not be terribly important to us. What will be important is the process itself.[2]

Other Dimensions: Prophets and Stewards

Our discussion of making disciples and apostles would be incomplete without the inclusion of two other goals of youth evangelization: the forming of prophets and the forming of stewards. A prophet is not someone who predicts the future. Instead, he or she is a person of emerging gospel truth. Perhaps this is best explained through the following story.

One day, a campus minister asked my advice about how best to engage high school students in prophetic conversation—to get them to take gospel stands and then articulate them. I advised her to gently nudge her students toward convictions—values from which they could not budge, beliefs they would be willing to die for. I added that what was also needed was the transformation of anger. In order to be a prophet, the person must speak the truth and others must be willing to hear the message. Nothing impedes prophecy more than a person who is angry. Shrill anger repels listeners more than it attracts followers.

---

[2] A more practical view of forming disciples and apostles will be shared in Chapter 9, "Full-Cycle Organic-Growth Youth Ministry."

In a culture that advises the middle class not to "make eye contact" with the less fortunate, perhaps the best way to form prophets is to expose young people to the dysfunctional aspects of society—the things that need changing. I recently gave a series of talks at a parish in Washington, D.C., that was dedicating a new social center and rectory. This parish is situated near the White House and other government shrines. One morning, as I left my comfortable hotel to go jogging, I was struck by the social contrasts I saw. On the one hand, I saw the rich hotel, the shining new parish buildings, and the multistory government buildings. On the other hand, I saw a number of people sleeping in a nearby park—in cold weather, on the grass, on park benches, with cardboard as a meager covering over them. Later at a parish meeting, a socially aware parishioner brought up these contrasts. He referred to the comfort and luxury of government and religion in the face of abject poverty and discouragement. He challenged parishioners to pay attention to homelessness and to do something about it. This man was acting as a prophet.

Jim Wallis (*Sojourners* magazine), Thomas Groome, and others have spoken and written at length about the relationship between proximity and justice. We need proximity to situations of injustice and suffering if we are to become people of conscience and justice. While the development of critical reflection skills in our young people is important, it is not enough. We must also give young people opportunities—under supervision—to witness first-hand both the plight of the poor and the heroic efforts being made by some people to help them.

A healthy spirituality for young people should also involve some experience in discerning the charisms, or gifts, that a young person has that can be shared for the common good and the glory of God. This is what I mean by a spirituality of stewardship. I shall discuss this spirituality further in the next chapter.

7

Youth, Spiritual Direction, and Stewardship

I n Chapter 5, I discussed the need for multiple-leader ministries in a small intergenerational youth community. Among the adult ministers, some leaders should be skilled in organization. These leaders should help facilitate the social and administrative details of the group's life, as well as its participation in the wider youth community's social and administrative issues. At least one adult leader ought to have catechetical skills in breaking open God's word and handing on the faith tradition in a relevant way. Some adult in the group also needs to be skilled in spiritual direction.[1]

Spiritual direction makes evangelization and catechesis practical, in that it helps a young person develop a liveable spirituality. Spiritual direction is not so much something you give to, or do for, someone. Rather, the spiritual director helps the young person discover his or her own spiritual direction in life. Spiritual direction is unique, based on the personality of each individual. I believe a fault in past religious education programs has been the attempt to make all young people live out one style of spirituality. Often, this spirituality was of an introverted, otherworldly style. In response to such force-fed spiritual methodologies, many young people have naturally rebelled and

---

[1] The spiritual director need not be an additional person from the leaders already mentioned. The spiritual director may be someone in another ministry in the group.

resisted. Their negative reactions have been interpreted as disinterest in spiritual realities, but nothing could be further from the truth. The real truth is: Young people do not want to be pushed around. They want to live inside their own questions and issues, through the lens of their God-given individuality and subjectivity. They should not be denied this.

In the process of full-cycle youth evangelization, spiritual direction often needs to take place later on in the process. While younger adolescents could perhaps take small bits of it, spiritual direction presupposes some depth, or maturity, of faith—some deeper level of searching, some willingness on the part of the young person to move on a deeper level of commitment. Spiritual direction also presupposes that a parallel level of depth and growth is taking place in the director.

One of the values of spiritual direction in the evangelization-catechetical process is that a young person does not just hear about God, faith, and Church (the language of religion). Rather, the young person encounters another human being who incarnates the Gospel. The spiritual director becomes, in a sense, another Christ. He or she gives witness that the Christian life is possible. The director also witnesses to his or her own life-changing relationship with God and the Christian community.

Meetings between the young person and the spiritual director ought to be of sufficient frequency that they develop a significant relationship. In preparation for being a spiritual director, the adult needs training in basic relational skills such as active listening, empathy, confrontation, conflict resolution, effective questions, and nondefensiveness when personally challenged. Five other skills are also required: teaching a person to pray, focusing, discernment of charisms, discernment of spirits, and forming disciples and good citizens. In the sections that follow, I will briefly discuss each of these five skills.

Teaching a Person to Pray

We can give young people no greater gift than to awaken in them the ability to pray. Through evangelization and spiritual direction, we need to lead young people to experience prayer as a growth in communion with themselves, God, and others. Indeed, the only way to teach prayer is experientially. When the apostles asked Jesus to teach them to pray, he did not give them a talk on prayer. Instead, he prayed with them. Likewise, spiritual direction ought to give a young person a taste of all kinds of praying:

- *Traditional, memorized prayers.* These prayers are especially helpful when the young person experiences fatigue, anxiety, or other circumstances in which "other words won't come."

- *Spontaneous, personal prayer.* Because such prayers are self-revealing, the director must take the lead and give example. The director can nudge a young person toward spontaneous prayer by initially keeping such prayers simple—often in the form of short petitions.

- *Praying with Scripture.* Praying with Scripture initially requires a lot of direction. Young people need to be encouraged to enter imaginatively into a gospel passage—to become a character in a gospel scene, to personalize the encounter, and then to speak to God about whatever strikes them regarding the passage.

- *Journal writing.* Writing has a wonderful potential for objectifying and clarifying one's inner world. Keeping a journal can be especially helpful in life situations of confusion or pain, when we are trying to chart some course for the future. Journal writing can become more prayerful if it is directed to God in the form of a letter.

- *Meditation.* Religious educator Maria Harris speaks of the importance of using the confrontative imagination in religious education. The confrontative imagination reflects on and scrutinizes a specific issue. The confrontative imagination is used in meditative exercises in which we help young people reflect on certain aspects of their own lives, the world around them, a passage from or word from Scripture, a brief prayerful line repeated over and over again. Sitting, walking, being in nature, or breathing exercises are effective techniques for getting into meditation.

- *Contemplation.* Hopefully, different types of prayer opportunities will lead a young person to the experience of contemplation—a peaceful oneness with God. In a rushed society where "trophy" children are pushed quickly from one achieving experience to another, most American young people have had little or no experience with contemplation. One way to introduce young people to contemplation is to have them take a word or phrase or one-line prayer and repeat it verbally or mentally over and over again, often timed with breathing. Two examples of short prayers that can lead to contemplation are the Jesus prayer ("Lord Jesus, Son of the living God, have mercy on me, a sinner") and Jesus' own prayer on the cross ("Father, into your hands, I hand over my life").

One of the most positive experiences I had on a youth retreat was an experience of meditation-contemplation. In planning the retreat, the coordinating committee took the risk of scheduling one full hour of "alone time" in the midst of a busy schedule of talks and group activities. During this hour, the young people were asked to go to their rooms, to spend a little time gazing at themselves in the mirror, and then to speak to God about the status of their lives. At the end of the hour, the coordinating committee played a contemporary song about human growth (via loudspeakers) into each young person's room. Upon returning to the large group after sixty minutes alone, the young people were subdued and reflective. Many of them (who were juniors and seniors, true veterans of many youth retreats) described their time alone as the most powerful retreat experience they had ever had.

Focusing

Eugene Gendlin, in his book *Focusing,* maintains that much of what we go to counselors and therapists for, we can do for ourselves. Gendlin is speaking of the ability to focus—to go within ourselves and get in touch with the deepest parts of our spiritual selves. Gendlin's steps for focusing, for getting in touch with ourselves, are simple:

1. *Create a space.* In the busyness of life, we must find time and space for focusing.
2. *Let the mind roam.* Rather than always controlling our thoughts, we must let our minds wander to wherever they take us.
3. *Begin to name feelings.* So many young people (especially males) have not fully developed the ability to name their feelings. Naming is important. If not properly labeled, feelings can become powerful forces with destructive powers.
4. *Get a body sense.* Young people should be encouraged to get in touch with how different feelings (anger, jealousy, sadness, love) make their bodies feel.

5. *Check for precision.* In this last step, we try to get ever more precise in naming and labeling what is going on inside of us.

Gendlin and others working his system say that too many of us engage in "process-skipping." We do the minimum in order to get through a certain process. As a result, we fail to focus well on our interior dynamics. To the degree that we do process-skipping, we run the risk of becoming diverted into addictive, self-destructive types of behavior.

It has been my experience—both in my own personal spirituality and in offering spiritual direction to others—that focusing exercises can greatly enrich one's prayer life. I encourage my directees, after they have focused on an amount of material, to lift that interior material up in prayer. Prayerful focusing is like standing emotionally naked before God, being totally one's self. Adolescents who have strong emotional swings can benefit greatly from these exercises. Adding the God-spiritural dimension to their reality assures them of an ever-loving Companion who will never abandon them.

Ann Wilson Schaef's book, *Beyond Therapy, Beyond Science,* speaks of the need we all have to "work the deep process of our lives." A deep process is an unresolved emotional issue or crisis. Often, tears, dreams, spontaneous memories, panic attacks, and waves of sadness or depression can act as doorways into such work. Schaef says that it is vital to notice these doorways and enter them. Such entrance will often involve strong emotional catharsis, but will also result in healing and learning. I believe that focusing and deep process work are important new psychological contributions to an improving, deepening prayer life.

Discernment of Charisms

In seminars and missions I have given around the country, I have spoken of our need to get away from "Price Is Right" ministry. In that television game show, contestants are invited to "come on down" to participate in the game? In a similar way, clerics and staff members frequently stand at a microphone on Sunday morning pleading for more volunteers to "come on down" to fill the vacancies that exist in parish programming. Good-hearted, generous people dedicate time and energy for ministries they have barely explored. They jump into a task for which they may not be gifted. Two dangers in such "Price Is Right" ministry are burnout (because one is not suited for the ministry) and "rustout" (because the ministry does not use one's gifts).

As I have said before in this book, youth evangelization necessitates a diversity of ministries. Both adult ministers and adolescent peer ministers need to discern their own giftedness in order to insure a "good fit" between minister and ministry. This discernment of charisms has deeper implications. Spiritual directors/mentors need to help the young people they are directing to discover their giftedness and then to use those gifts in the Christian community.

A central issue, which is ignored by many archdiocesan administrative centers, is the vocation of the ordinary baptized Catholic. Although Vatican II emphasized baptismal spirituality and the vocation of ALL the People of God, we as Church are still investing money and personnel in the recruitment and training of priests and religious. Despite heroic efforts, the slide in such vocations continues. James Fowler, in *Becoming Adult, Becoming Christian,* raises this issue regarding the vocation of all people. He insists that God calls each person in a unique direction, based on his or her gifts and the needs of the world. Fowler puts it succinctly: A vocation is the marriage of a person's giftedness to the needs and wounds of the world. True vocation ministry is not just about priests and religious sisters and brothers; it is about helping all people listen to God's call.

In an earlier chapter, I talked about Erik Erikson's metaphor of the adolescent as "life apprentice." I think Erikson's metaphor is a useful one, especially when applied to spiritual direction of young people. Relative to vocation, spiritual directors need to help young people with the following tasks:

1. *Discern and sort out their gifts, charisms, or their sharing in the Holy Spirit's power.* Such discernment is done by helping young people name the positive attributes or talents they have, as well as their values, virtues, and strengths in temperament. The spiritual director needs to listen to the self-analysis of young people and then give feedback. In seminars on discernment, I call this process "listening to one's inner world," and "seeking out the confirmation/affirmation of people who represent a credible outer world."

2. *Encouragement in a discouraging world.* Young people, like most of us, are aware of "the holes in the Swiss cheese." That is, they are acutely aware of what is wrong with them. They need to have the "cheese," the good that they are, pointed out to them. Those of us who are trained in the skills of Adlerian counseling and psychotherapy had this principle drummed into us. We are to encourage others. Encouragement is not flip, phoney praise. In spiritual direction, encouragement means holding up an imaginary mirror to young people and helping them see what is good and beautiful about themselves. This task of encouragement demands that the spiritual director take serious time to reflect on the life and personality of each young person with whom he or she works, in order to give accurate, life-giving feedback.

3. *Experience ministry firsthand.* Most people who have prepared for pastoral ministry will tell you that classroom input and study did not have as much impact on them as did their internship or in-service experience. Some people say the classroom material was valuable, but that it really did not fall into place until it was joined to concrete experiences of ministry and service. Similarly, young people need to have some proximity to and experience with the various dimensions of need in the world. Working in soup kitchens, spending time with the homeless, visiting the sick and the elderly are not just "more busy stuff" for the youth worker and young people. These activities need to be presented in the context of vocation.

4. *Reflect on experiences.* Young people need to reflect on and process the field experiences they have. While this reflecting can be done one-on-one between spiritual director and adolescent, there is an even greater richness when the reflecting is done in a small group. As Thomas Groome says, reflecting on his shared praxis, God's Spirit is moving in all the small group members. The "animator" must become a facilitator, easing the way for God's wisdom to emerge in the collective wisdom of the small group.

Discernment of Spirits

The need for a discernment of spirits (the discernment of what is or is not of the Gospel) was alluded to in the previous chapter. I am becoming increasingly convinced that we cannot run from the world. If the Gospel is to take root in young people, then our area, our laboratory, needs to be the world. In the future, all youth evangelization must be inculturation. The Gospel must merge with a native culture—in our case, American consumer-oriented, middle-class culture. In an inculturation process, we need to look at our culture for gospel-friendly values that advance God's Reign. We also need to be sensitive to the culture's anti-Christ values, which dilute or weaken the Gospel.

On October 30, 1992, Jesuit Father John Kavanaugh presented a conference at St. John's University in New York. At the conference, Kavanaugh gave examples of the anti-gospel force in American culture. He said that advertising—both on television and in other aspects of media—leads people away from the sense of human personhood to the perception of object-reality. In this perception, to be "real" is to be an "object." Thus, lust replaces chastity, power replaces obedience, money replaces poverty, and corporate life replaces familial-interpersonal relationships. The effect of such advertising is becoming apparent: Greed and consumption are becoming the dominant images out of which many people live. Human values and human identity are in need of massive reconstruction. Thus, part of the youth evangelization effort must involve the transmission of skills for critiquing the dominant culture and acting on gospel values.

Reacting to Cardinal Roger Mahoney's recent criticism of the media, Thomas E. Blackburn of the *National Catholic Reporter* wrote rather soberly, "Values determine movies, and people with money determine values." Blackburn encouraged his readers to understand and become critical of our capitalist system, which is increasingly antihuman in its entertainment. Implicit in Blackburn's article is this realization: If we, as American Christians, stop giving our money to such entertainment-oriented displays of anti-human values, the industry might begin to shrivel.

In the diocese of Rochester, New York, a priest recently told me the story of one high school boy who was adopted. A controversy broke out in one of the boy's classes regarding the rightness or wrongness of abortion. One young woman said clearly that she was pro-choice and would choose to abort if she became pregnant. The adopted boy, however, explained to the class that he was against abortion and was quite happy that his mother chose to carry him to full term and then offer him to the adoption process, which ultimately resulted in his placement with his current family. The boy's personal testimony created a hush in the classroom, and the young woman broke into tears. This high school boy certainly had taken a strong stand against the culture's media and advertising. He was prophetic in witnessing to the Gospel's option for life.

Forming Disciples and Good Citizens

Thomas Groome has described the role of parishes as "reflective communities of action." In evangelizing, catechizing, and directing young people, we need to break down the dichotomy between Church and world, between Church and reality. We need to help young people realize that "sanctuary ministries" (ministries on the altar) are not the most important work of the Church. Instead, the most pressing goal of contemporary Christianity is to bring Jesus Christ to the world through family, work, friendship, discipleship, and apostleship. Pope Paul VI spoke of evangelization as no less than this—the transformation of society through the power of the Gospel. I believe that young people who are good apostles and disciples will ultimately become good, responsible citizens.

The Role of the Spiritual Companion

Obviously, I place high value on the importance of the spiritual director's role in the lives of young people. This comes, I believe, from my experience with the Order of Initiation, where the role of the sponsor, or spiritual companion, is considered vital. This role was important in the catechumenal process and structures of the early Church. The sponsor was the minister who was intimately involved in discernment of the conversion process. The sponsor even had a liturgical role in presenting the candidate to the larger liturgical assembly.[2]

Similarly, today's spiritual director acts as a spiritual companion to young people as they undergo the process of conversion. A related topic,

---

[2] In all of the suggested activities of the spiritual director, the director may be working one-on-one with an individual or with a FLAME group.

which will be discussed in the next chapter, concerns the preparation of young people for Confirmation. When in the conversion process should the young person be confirmed? How can we convey to young people the continued need for evangelization and spiritual direction once Confirmation has taken place?

— 8 —

The Confirmation Controversy

When I first began doing youth evangelization twenty years ago, its emphasis was on commitment and personal responsibility for one's faith. Confirmation was a "piece" of the process. The process, which resembled a catechumenal journey, consisted first of a period of evangelization (social ministry programs and basic spiritual seeking). Evangelization led to a period of catechesis (learning opportunities using different modules), based on subjective needs and questions of young people. Catechesis, in turn, led to a period of spiritual direction that included many of the dynamics discussed in the previous chapter. Spiritual direction was, in effect, "proximate preparation" for celebrating Confirmation with integrity. No age was set *a priori* for the celebration. When (and if) young people felt so called and had completed some basic requirements, they celebrated the sacrament.

The theology of Confirmation that we advocated was multilayered. At no time did we say that Confirmation was a celebration of becoming an adult in the Church. (That simply was, and is not, true. Psychologically and spiritually, an adolescent is not an adult. To ritualize this is liturgical dishonesty.) Instead, we taught that the sacrament of Confirmation celebrated the following:

- the completion of one's initiation into the Church;
- the owning of one's faith, given at Baptism;
- the taking of responsibility for one's faith;

- the serious discernment of charisms to be used in ministry throughout life;
- and the celebration of personal Pentecost—awakening to the power and influence of the Holy Spirit in one's life.

While some young people minimally approached the process, significant numbers of young people took the process very seriously. Confirmations resembled ordinations in their sense of responsibility and commitment. Perhaps the process and the sacramental celebration demanded more of the adolescents than they were developmentally capable of. Nonetheless, the process temporarily assured young people of a safety zone in the larger world of peer pressure, drugs, and heightened sexual activity.

Like many parish ministers, my consciousness regarding Confirmation has been raised in the last few years. Although I have operated out of initiation spirituality for twenty years, initiation has certainly become more of a filter, or lens, through which I now approach religious education. I also have become aware that, because Confirmation has been a sacrament looking for a theology,[1] many people in pastoral ministry have used the rite to promote their own biases.

Confusion about the theology of Confirmation and the "proper age" for its celebration has persisted. Let us attempt to sift through some of the biases and issues present in the Confirmation controversy.

The "Traditional Order" Proponents

People who espouse the traditional order for celebrating initiation (Baptism, Confirmation, Eucharist), hold to the following points:
- Baptism, Confirmation, and Eucharist are initiation rites.
- Both adults and children should celebrate the Sacraments of Initiation in the traditional order—Baptism, Confirmation, Eucharist. Normally, these sacraments should be celebrated in one ceremony.

---

[1] Much research has been done on the history of Confirmation. It seems there was a gradual separation between the rite by which the bishop laid on hands and anointed catechumens and the Rite of Baptism. Eventually, Confirmation became a separate sacrament with a theological conviction that a new, different experience of the Holy Spirit came through the sacrament. In 1274, the Council of Lyons made this separate pastoral practice "official." Pope Pius X changed the usual order of initiation (Baptism, Confirmation, Eucharist) when, in the encyclical *Quam Singulari* (1905), he encouraged those who reached the age of reason (seven) to celebrate First Eucharist. But even the renewal of the Rite of Confirmation in 1971 did little to solidify pastoral practice regarding the sacrament.

- Confirmation is a commission for Eucharist—communion at the Table of the Lord.
- One possible pastoral strategy is to follow the Byzantine/Orthodox practice of celebrating Confirmation at the time of infant Baptism. (This practice, however, is not supported by Canon Law.)
- Another pastoral practice is to have Confirmation and Eucharist in rapid sequence, at the age of seven, in the original order.[2]

The "Later Age" Proponents

People who espouse celebrating Confirmation at a later age hold to the following points:
- Adolescence and young adulthood are more psychologically congruent with the stage in the life span that is recommended for Confirmation by the Order of Initiation.
- Confirmation is the completion of the process of initiation. It is, or should be, a volitional act. For this reason, it should be optional.
- Confirmation is a transition ritual, a rite of passage. This transition is one from relative passivity to an active commitment to service.[3]

The Greatest Pastoral Good

Currently, initiation spirituality and theology are calling for a restored order of initiation (Baptism, Confirmation, then Eucharist). Some parishes and dioceses are encouraging Confirmation before Eucharist, at the age of reason. I personally do not see "traditional order" as the greatest need regarding Confirmation. Instead, my concerns are these: Where does this rite do the greatest pastoral good? Where does it seem that Confirmation might be celebrated with the greatest honesty and integrity?

---

[2] Canon 788 of the 1918 Code of Canon Law set age seven as the normative age for Confirmation. Thus, the latter pastoral strategy is more acceptable in Catholic culture than the Byzantine/Orthodox practice. The age of discretion (age seven) was further supported by the 1971 Rite of Confirmation (no. 11), the 1972 version of the Order of Initiation (no. 34), the 1988 revision of the Order of Initiation, and the 1983 Code of Canon Law (no. 891). Whole dioceses—such as Spokane, Washington, and Greensburg, Pennsylvania—have switched to an age seven Confirmation-Eucharist praxis.

[3] Pope Paul VI spoke of a unique experience of the Holy Spirit that Confirmation provided. He regarded Confirmation as a rite of becoming a full adult member of the Church. The late pope also spoke of Confirmation as a commissioning, or missioning, in order to utilize the gifts of the Spirit in bringing the Gospel to the world.

Some people have suggested that it would be good if the Church abandoned infant Baptism as a common practice and postponed initiation in all of its ritual expressions until adulthood, when one can freely choose how to live one's faith and spirituality. I would certainly support such a change. Parishes would have to devise for infants and their parents new rituals of welcome into the faith family. Religious education would no longer be a sacramental "assembly line" that one leaves at the age of fourteen. Instead, religious education from childhood to adolescence would be a kind of pre-catechumenate. Catechesis would begin to take place during the teen years. I think that parish religious education programs, parents' involvement in the faith lives of their children, the vibrancy of parish spirituality would all change drastically by delaying Baptism, Confirmation, and Eucharist to the young adult years.

Having said this, let me add that such a shift is not likely to happen soon. Meanwhile, we in pastoral ministry and religious education must be responsible for creating a milieu, or environment, around Confirmation and all sacraments so that there is a greater likelihood of faith growth, spiritual transformation, and conversion. Following this line of reasoning, and leaning heavily on the theological convictions that Confirmation is the completion of initiation and a personal/communal Pentecost experience, I believe it still can be argued that Confirmation can be a pastoral good in ministry to adolescents. The key to good youth ministry, however, is NOT high school Confirmation. Rather, what we need is organically growing, full-cycle youth evangelization. Confirmation can be a ritual moment in this overall process. But other rituals (baptism in the Holy Spirit, renewal of one's baptismal promises, commissioning rites) can also be devised to help young people publicly own their faith.

Archbishop Weakland, in a recent Catholic newspaper column, wrote that he needed further prayer, study, and dialogue before he would consider radically altering his policy regarding Confirmation. He will encourage his parishes, therefore, to "stay the course" with adolescent or young adult celebration of the sacrament. I think his approach of prayerful discernment is a good praxis for all of us in youth ministry to adopt. Sacraments should be celebrations of conversion and religious experience. Any process of catechesis and formation leading up to a sacramental moment ought to facilitate a genuine experience of such profound realities.

9

Full-Cycle Organic-Growth Youth Ministry

As I stated earlier, the vision for youth ministry espoused in this book is teleological, or purposive. A youth ministry effort ought to call young people to a convicted life, to commitment. Another tenet of this book is that youth ministry ought to be about long-term care, about companioning young people (to the degree this is possible) from the intermediate grades through young adulthood. A third major belief of this book is that local churches ought not to buy into prepackaged total youth ministry programs, but rather, "organically grow" their own programs through a multiplicity of resources. Related to these three principles are two others, which I referred to in my book *The Evangelizing Parish*.

- *Maximum influence.* A parish or cluster of parishes has the responsibility to contact and reach as many young people as possible. This responsibility is not a "numbers game"; it is, rather, a Gospel mandate to reach out to the entire world.
- *Multiplication of ministers.* The only way this can be done is if the "youth minister" acts as a "coordinator of youth ministries," and thereby multiplies the number of people doing effective youth evangelization.

Having reviewed these five underlying principles, let us try to synthesize the material of previous chapters in a holistic vision. To do this, we will note the parallels between the catechumenate, evangelical youth ministry, and the FLAME process of youth evangelization.

The Catechumenate

Many of us are familiar with the dynamics of the catechumenate, or the Order of Initiation. To facilitate the process of conversion, the Order suggests the following ministerial efforts, which may be adapted when pastorally appropriate or necessary.

The Order of Initiation

Pre-Catechumenate (A Time for Evangelization)
- reach-out and relational bonding
- invitation to, and first taste of, community
- listening to and responding to basic life searches and questions
- initial proclamation of the Good News
- building on the spirituality apparent in one's life thus far
- theological reflection that puts one in touch with God present in human experience
- the beginning of sponsorship
- responding to basic questions about Church culture—giving an overview of Church devotional/liturgical customs, Church art and environment
- writing spiritual autobiographies
- initial interview with staff and team
- discernment of conversion

Rite of Acceptance into the Order of Catechumens (for the unbaptized)
    OR
Rite of Welcome
    (for the already baptized who seek full communion with the Church)[1]

Catechumenate (A Time for Learning)
- awakened faith seeks fulfillment and expansion
- God's word and Church tradition are systematically presented through the lens of the liturgical year and the subjective needs and questions of the catechumens/candidates

---

[1] Both rituals take place in the weekend eucharistic assembly.

- immersion into community and apprenticing in ministry/mission
- continued discernment of conversion
- further clarification of Church, culture, practice, art, environment, devotion, and liturgy
- while evangelizers and sponsors continue to serve, the ministry of catechesis prevails

Rite of Election (for the unbaptized)
　　OR
Call to Conversion (for the already baptized)[2]

Purification and Enlightenment
　(The Lenten Journey before Celebration of Initiation)
- continued ministries of witnessing, sponsoring, and catechesis
- special emphasis on spiritual direction and discipleship
- prayerful scrutinies and prayers of exorcism for liberation from all that impedes conversion
- liturgical/catechetical focus on the creed and the Lord's Prayer as models of core convictions and prayer
- continued discernment of conversion

Sacraments of Initiation
　(Celebration of One's Vows to God and the Catholic Community)
- celebration of Baptism (for the unbaptized)
- celebration of Confirmation
- celebration of Eucharist

Mystagogia (Follow-up to Initiation)
- continued evangelization, catechesis, and guidance
- time for further catechesis on the sacramental life; a reflection on all that has happened thus far
- time for further discernment of charisms and finding one's place in the community

---

[2] Both rituals take place in the eucharistic assembly.

Recent efforts by the North American Forum on the Catechumenate and others have tried to reimage the Order of Initiation NOT in a linear model, but in a circular model (see Figure 1).

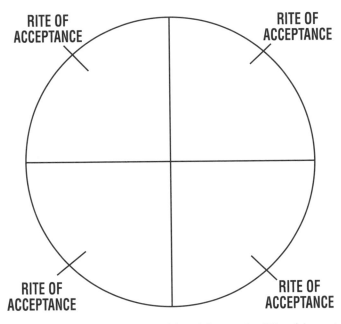

Figure 1. In a circular model, the parish celebrates the Rite of Acceptance into the Catechumenate four or more times a year, when a significant number have gathered for inquiry.

In this circular model, the parish celebrates the Rite of Acceptance into the Catechumenate four or more times a year, as opposed to the previous practice of celebrating the rite once a year, each autumn. The flexibility of the circular model allows prospective catechumens to begin the initiation process when they are ready. A new group of catechumens begins when there is a sufficient number of people to constitute a small faith-sharing group. Granted, the circular model of initiation is messy. Rather than following a clean programmatic design, the circular model is based on discernment, with people moving to the next stage only when they are discerned ready. Likewise, proximate preparation for the sacraments (purification and enlightenment) begins when individuals are discerned ready for this Lenten "leg" of the journey. In other words, some catechumens may be discerned ready to enter proximate preparation for the sacraments the first Lent after they have been accepted into the catechumenate. Other catechumens may not reach this discernment until the second or third Lent after acceptance into the catechumenate (see Figure 2).

Figure 2. In the circular model, catechumens and candidates choose, upon discernment with sponsor and team, when to begin purification and enlightenment, in preparation for reception of the sacraments.

In order to work, the circular model necessitates the multiplication of many ministries and ministers.

Evangelical Youth Ministry

In studying the many evangelical models of youth ministry, I have found them all to follow a similar plan, despite what they might popularly call each stage.

Evangelical Models of Youth Ministry

Stage One: The emphasis is on fun and social relationships and the beginnings of small group community.

Stage Two: A young person staying with the process becomes sensitized to and aware of the realities of the spiritual life.

Stage Three: A young person intentionally seeks out the means to become Christian and to deepen his or her faith.

Stage Four: A young person consciously becomes a disciple of Jesus, with an emphasis on personal relating with Jesus and commitment to the Church. (Often, a ritual—such as water baptism or baptism in the Holy Spirit—takes place here.)

Stage Five: A young person, having taken a journey of conversion that is often years in unfolding, makes a commitment to use his or her gifts as a worker for Christ (ministry).

All of these stages occur in small communities. During Stage Three, the young person takes on membership in an additional small community, one focused on deeper prayer and Scripture. Then, in Stage Five, a young person assumes leadership for younger adolescents who are in earlier stages of the process; or he or she assumes a ministerial role in the adult Church. Intergenerational ministers, unpaid and nonprofessional, are involved in the various stages of the process.

Notice the similarities in the five stages of the evangelical models and the Order of Initiation. Both processes emphasize the small group. Both processes are energized by the same five principles: teleology, long-term care, organic growth, multiplication of ministers, and maximum influence.

The FLAME Process of Youth Evangelization

FLAME is a Catholic interdenominational or nondenominational vision/strategy for youth evangelization. The letters stand for the following: Friendship, Leadership, Acceptance, Ministry, and Education. FLAME synthesizes the stages found in the Order of Initiation and the evangelical models of youth ministry. St. John Neumann Parish in St. Charles, Illinois, has further defined the FLAME model to look like this:

FLAME

Stage One: Discovery (Evangelization)
- outreach to teens through social events and activities
- involvement of adult and peer social ministers

Stage Two: Advance (Catechesis)
- social ministries continue
- learning modules that involve adult catechists

Stage Three: Discipleship (Spiritual Direction)
- social ministries continue
- catechesis continues
- one-on-one meetings with adult spiritual directors

Stage Four: Celebration (Confirmation)
- social ministries continue
- catechesis continues
- one-on-one meetings with spiritual directors continue
- public celebration of Confirmation, which involves liturgical ministers
- or some other public ritual of owning one's faith

Stage Five: Continuing the Journey (Follow-up)
- all previous ministries continue
- ongoing formation and nurturance
- active ministry in the Christian community

With the FLAME model, some clarification is needed for the term "organic growth." In organic growth, the coordinator of youth ministries works with a small group of peer and intergenerational leaders in sharing the vision and strategies for full-cycle youth evangelization. Eventually, that core group emerges as a team of leaders who, in turn, reach out and start their own small groups. The coordinator is responsible for providing the new leaders with names and prospects for such future groups. The coordinator also serves as a support and trainer in launching the groups. The real work, however, is done by the emerging teen and adult leaders.

In the FLAME process, an ideal intergenerational small community might consist of an adult evangelization/social life minister, an adult catechetical minister, an adult spiritual director, an adolescent small-group leader, an adolescent co-leader, an adolescent social life minister, an adolescent liturgical minister, an adolescent retreat coordinator minister, and an adolescent fund-raising minister. These roles, of course, could be combined; two roles, perhaps, could be handled by one person. Indeed, the list of adolescent ministries can be as long as the needs discerned by each small community.

Continuing with the idea of organic growth, the small community replicates itself many times in a multiplying network of small communities (see Figure 3).

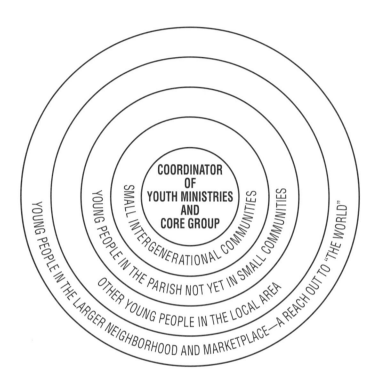

Figure 3. An organically growing small community is replicated many times in a network of small communities.

All individuals and small communities would be at different parts of the conversion journey—evangelization, catechesis, discipleship, celebrating, and continuing the journey.

Anyone who senses that organic-growth youth ministry has intrinsic value needs to keep in mind that the basic goal is outreach—especially to fringe young people, to the inactive and the unchurched. Thus, the original group, which consists of the coordinator of youth ministries, the adult ministers, and the adolescent core group, gradually becomes a network of small groups (see Figure 4).

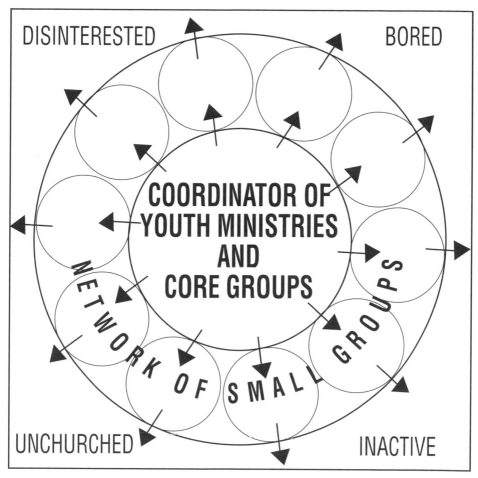

Figure 4. In the FLAME model, the original core group gradually becomes a network of small groups that reaches out to inactive or unchurched young people.

The goal of outreach is to invite the "outer rim" young people to a small group or a social activity sponsored by a small group or a network of groups.

A monthly calendar for a FLAME movement might look like this:

FLAME Large Group and Small Community Calendar

	Mon.	Tues.	Weds.	Thurs.	Fri.	Sat.	Sun.
Week 1				Large COR meeting of all groups (social, business, spiritual)		Social Event (open to all)	
Week 2	Small groups meet						
Week 3					Retreat (open)		
Week 4	Small groups meet						Discipleship groups

Notice that this calendar offers a variety of activities—from the social event (with outreach potential) to the discipleship group (for those well along in the journey). The heart of the whole movement is the weekly COR large group gathering. COR is the "entrance point" to the program. The COR evening is characterized by social, business, and spirituality time in individual small groups or with interacting small groups. At COR, the members are invited to do outreach to bring new members to their small group. Often a healthy competition develops among the groups for new membership. The two major outreach tools among the groups are the regular weekly COR meeting and the monthly social events. Retreats can also be an outreach opportunity, depending on their emphasis.[3]

More needs to be said about Stage Five (follow-up) in the FLAME process. We will discuss this stage further in the next chapter.

---

[3] Basic "Evangelization 101" retreats are ideal for "fringe" young people. However, overnights or retreats of a catechetical nature are often geared toward a more advanced group.

— 10 —

Stage Five: Follow-up

T he evangelical world speaks of "closing the back door" after someone has "come in the front door," lest the newcomer quickly enter the church and leave it. While such talk may sound flip or manipulative, these Christians are speaking about a truth. Church groups often lose people because of poor follow-through. For years, catechumenate ministers have lamented that new adult members will not come back for mystogogia after they have received the Sacraments of Initiation at the Easter Vigil. Part of the reason for this decline in participation is due to the fact that we are still locked into a fall-spring method of "doing parish." Indeed, why would new members come back for continued formation, when the rest of the parish is shutting down for the summer?

Unfortunately, much of what we do in religious education reflects a graduation mind-set. We accomplish a certain number of requirements over the span of a certain amount of time, and then we are done. Conventional religious education programs for young people are energized by the goal line—eighth grade graduation, the sacrament of Confirmation, or whatever is the catechetical "carrot." The goal is to complete the program. Upon completion, there often is an "in-between-the-times" drop-out period from Church, until the next sacrament, or carrot, is needed or required.

This graduation day approach is certainly evident in youth ministry, especially when it is intertwined with preparation for Confirmation. That is why I emphasize that FLAME—full-cycle youth evangelization—is NOT a high school Confirmation program. If a young person chooses to ritualize the completion of initiation by celebrating Confirmation, that is certainly a good. But the FLAME program says that there can be other ways to symbolize conversion. Whole "herds" of young people ought not to be put on a sacramental assembly line or conveyor belt. Nor should they have to pretend—for bishops, parents, and parish staff—that something transformational is going on within them. When we engage in such assembly-line, graduation-oriented efforts, whose needs are being served? Often, I think, we who are in leadership roles in ministry are merely serving our own needs.

Good youth ministry requires follow-through and long-term care. Such care eventually results in "feeder systems." This means that junior high ministries flow into high school ministries, and high school ministries flow into young adult ministries. Young adult ministries, in turn, often result in four or five different types of ministry to the differing subgroups under the young adult umbrella.

Many different strategies can comprise effective follow-up ministry with adolescents and young adults. In the pages that follow, I will present some of these strategies, focusing on each age group separately.

Ministry to High School Juniors and Seniors

Anyone who has worked extensively with adolescents knows the marked developmental differences between high school upperclassmen and high school freshmen and sophomores. While some juniors and seniors serve as peer ministers to freshmen and sophomores in the FLAME program, I have also found that older adolescents need something for their own level. On the other hand, I believe it is a mistake to think that older teens need the programmatic regularity or structure that younger teens need.

One important strategy with juniors and seniors is to utilize adult learning skills. Chief among these skills is correct discernment of the teens' interests and needs. This discernment includes surveying approaches to learning, sharing, and getting together that the teens particularly enjoy. Discernment also includes finding days and times that are convenient for the teens to gather, based on their school, work, sports, and interpersonal schedules.

In my work, I have found several strategies to be effective with older teens. One strategy has been to have occasional breakfast discussions on Sunday mornings. Of course, because of busyness, such occasional breakfasts have to be scheduled well ahead of time. A second strategy has been to have occasional potluck dinner discussions. These potluck dinners can be held at the parish center or in someone's home. It is understood that those who come to the dinner will be out in sufficient time to make evening commitments. A third strategy has been junior-senior retreats that pay special attention to issues of this age group: intimacy, future work, going to college, etc.

I have been amazed that many juniors and seniors who have been with a given small group community for a couple of years, really do want to stay with these proven relationships. After they graduate from high school, these teens may have to change the amount of time that they can be with the youth ministry effort. Nevertheless, they still want to have some contact.

Many juniors, seniors, and high school graduates respond favorably to youth ministry "reunions." Although the reunions are largely social in nature, they serve well in renewing old friendships and in anchoring older adolescents in the parish church. The major motivation that brings older teens back (or, for that matter, for the first time) to a youth ministry group is the quality of the outreach and interpersonal network. Fine catechetical materials and audiovisual programs limp without the infrastructure of meaningful, evangelistic relationships.

Young Adult Ministry

As I mentioned earlier, ministries to a given age group will hopefully create "feeder systems" for the next chronological grouping. Ideally, good high school youth ministry flows into serious, deliberate attempts at young adult ministry.

I have found that the 18-22 subgroup of young adults benefits from various strategies developed by the Archdiocese of Chicago. Under the coordination of Father John Cusick and Ms. Kate DeVries, the Archdiocese has developed an effective young adult religious education series called "Theology on Tap."[1] The series fine-tunes adult religious education to the needs and questions of young adults. Under the program, the Archdiocesan Young Adult Office helps clusters of parishes organize a summer series of talks and workshops. The parishes in the cluster finance the speakers, who are effective pastoral ministers or people of faith in the marketplace. Thousands of young adults participate in the series yearly. One critique that I have about the series is that it is not enough! Four, five, or even six weeks of effective young adult ministry in the summer does not speak of the full-cycle vision of this book. Ideally, "Theology on Tap" ought to be held on a year-round basis. In addition, the series needs to be supplemented by other ministries.

John Cusick, Kate DeVries, Dawn Mayer Melendez, and I have also worked at piloting young adult missions on a regional basis, in clusters of parishes. A mission is a series of retreat-like evenings consisting of Scripture, preaching, music, and ritual. Using a format popular among mid-lifers and older adults, we have adapted the process to the tastes and styles of young adults. Interestingly, several times that we have offered the missions, we have held them on the Monday, Tuesday, and Wednesday of Holy Week; their central theme was the Paschal Mystery—life, death, and resurrection. The Holy Week mission had an additional goal of facilitating the movement of young adults into their parishes for a good experience of the Triduum (Holy Thursday, Good Friday, and the Easter Vigil).

Some dioceses in Australia have taken ongoing formation of young adults even further and more seriously. The Australian dioceses are multiplying small groups and communities of young adults. The groups, which very much have a catechumenal rhythm to them, are made up of spiritually-seeking young adults and older adult mentors. After a significant number of sessions, the process moves toward a retreat that encourages participants toward

---

[1] In placing this program under the 18-22 age category, I do not wish to shortchange the program's effectiveness at other stages of young adulthood. Since its inception over a decade ago, "Theology on Tap" has added a number of ministry strategies for each stage of young adulthood.

responsible Church membership. The Australian movement is called "Toward Discipleship." Its aim is to reach out to the many young adult Australian Catholics who are baptized, but are, at best, nominal Catholics.

To maintain contact with young adults who are away at school, some members of parish staffs have begun to visit college campuses. While traveling to some faraway campus is quite time-consuming, the ministers regard these visits as an important expression of our concern for and commitment to parish young people. While on campus, the ministers gather students from the parish or from local parishes, talk with them about their experience, and invite them and their new friends out for a meal. Other parishes, on a weekly basis, mail the parish bulletin to their college-bound parishioners. This is a relatively simple effort, but it provides a bridge between the students who are away and the faith community they have come from.

Some of the strategies just summarized, if adapted, could also be used for the other subgroups of young adults. The different age groups also benefit from marriage preparation, marriage enrichment, and opportunities for healing for those grieving a loss through death or divorce. As youth ministers, it is important to remember that what young adults want and respond to best is interest-based, or needs-based, religious education and ministry.

11

Important Issues in Ministering to Young People

A nyone working with young people should be particularly sensitive to special youth issues or concerns of the 1990s and beyond. Among these issues are cults and sects, alcohol and drug abuse, suicide, sexual activity, rock music and pop culture, and eating disorders. Pastoral ministers—both professionals and volunteers—do not have to be experts on these issues. But pastoral ministers should be alert to these issues and should be ready to make referrals to connect the young person in need with skilled people who can help. For this reason, I will briefly and separately discuss these issues in the following pages.

Cults and Sects
The word "proselytism" refers to the use of unfair, even coercive, practices to convince a person to leave one church for another. Proselytizing groups run a continuum from hard-core "mind control" groups (such as the "Moonies") to "soft sects" found in popular evangelical churches.[1]

---

[1] I believe that one reason Catholics of all ages are so prone to being manipulated by cults is the anemic version of evangelization and catechesis many of them have experienced over the last twenty-five to thirty years. In a word, young Catholics, specifically, are lacking in apologetics—the ability to verbalize or explain their faith. To the degree that young people are inarticulate about their faith, they are easily bowled over by well-scripted proselytizers and mainstream evangelicals.

Regarding cultic, sect-like movements in general, the Vatican issued a report in 1986 that analyzed the attraction of these groups to the general public, recent immigrants, racial-ethnic minorities, and young people. Other research on the American scene has also contributed to this sparse, but growing, wisdom. Here is a brief summary of that research:

1. *People in a vulnerable position are the most affected by cultic movements.* Such vulnerable people include the unemployed, racial or ethnic minority groups, those living far from an "organized religious church," those away from home on university campuses, and—in general—adolescents and young people.

2. *Cultic movements employ finely tuned strategies to attract and motivate followers.* "Love bombing" is the term commonly used to describe these strategies. "Love bombing" makes young people feel as if they are the most important people in the world. This especially appeals to people suffering from a poor self-concept, relational abuse, recent rejection, or loneliness.

3. *People tend to join cults for good reasons.* People who join cults tend to be seeking deep realities, such as belonging, truth, meaning, answers, identity, recognition, guidance, the transcendent, life-vision, and commitment.

4. *Cultic movements usually provide a ready way for new members to ascend quickly into leadership and responsibility.* This "upward mobility" appeals especially to people who do not think they can gain recognition for themselves in any other way.

While this summary does not do justice to the research on cults, it does seem to cry out for mainline churches (specifically the Catholic Church) to engage in radical self-renewal in order to "compete" with these movements. I believe this self-renewal would have the following components: small faith communities, better faith formation for young people, an emphasis on the ministries of healing and reconciliation, better worship, more inculturation efforts, and lay pastoring.

Without doubt, the most dangerous among the cultic movements in America are satanic groups. I say this because I have had several horrifying experiences with young people who were involved in satanic cults. Because of their involvement, these various young people were into ritualistic slaying of animals, self-immolation or self-wounding, obsessive fascination with heavy metal music, and—in one case—suicide.[2]

Father Eric Barr, a Newman chaplain at Northern Illinois University in DeKalb, Illinois, has divided satanic cults into the following three types:

- *Solitary satanists.* These people are usually high school age young people who tend not to "fit in." In retaliation for being rejected, they establish personalized satanic rituals for themselves.
- *New satanic churches.* These churches are recognized as "legitimate," and are even advertized in the yellow pages. Such churches preach the values of self-indulgence, power, and the accumulation of wealth. They see Satan as the embodiment of what it means to be human.
- *Outlaw cults.* This type of satanic cult is the most dangerous of the three. Outlaw cults actually worship Satan as "the evil one" of the New Testament. They advocate sadomasochism and sexually deviant behavior. Cult members participate in orgies for power and domination. Those populating these cults range in age (on the average) from fifteen to twenty-five. The most common crimes of these satanists include thefts of consecrated hosts and sacred vessels from Christian churches, damaging property with satanic graffiti, grave robberies, animal sacrifice, and human sacrifice.

I include this material to round out our discussion of youth issues and also to tip off youth workers to symptomatic behavior in young people that might be indicative of more serious, life-threatening problems.

Alcohol and Drug Abuse

Many of the young people I worked with in the 1970s and 1980s experimented with heavy drugs. I spent some long hours in emergency rooms, praying that those who had overdosed would recover. My prayers were not always answered.

Because many teenagers are naturally subject to mood swings, substance abuse among them can be hard to discern. Yet, there are some telling "signs" in adolescents and young adults that should alert youth ministers to possible

---

[2] This suicide was motivated by the young man's wish to "get to the other side," to gain power so that he might come back and seek revenge on the peers who had mocked and hurt him.

substance abuse. These signs include erratic behavior, isolation, personality changes, decline in performance, and denial.

Alcohol abuse alone kills more Americans each year than AIDS. Indeed, alcoholism is the number three health problem in the United States. One-third of the U.S. population is negatively influenced by people who abuse alcohol. Alcoholism is a great masquerader, often manifesting itself in a variety of other disease-like symptoms: anxiety attacks, panic disorder, depression, etc. As youth ministers, we have to be careful that we are not treating these symptoms without also addressing the real problem—the substance abuse.

A recent study by the Health and Human Services Department reported that eight million teenagers (more than one-third of the nation's teenage population) drink alcohol weekly. Nearly half a million teens are binge drinkers; these teens consume an average of fifteen drinks each week. About 5.4 million teens have consumed five or more consecutive drinks on at least one occasion. Many of these adolescents are alcoholic already.

The same study found that the number of young people using marijuana, cocaine, and other hard drugs is declining. But alcohol use and heavy drinking remain high. Of the teenagers who drink, the study found that thirty-one percent sometimes drink alone, forty-one percent drink when they are upset, twenty-five percent drink when they get bored, and twenty-five percent drink specifically to get high. Among the binge drinkers (those averaging fifteen drinks per week), thirty-nine percent drink alone, fifty-eight percent drink when they are upset, thirty percent drink when they are bored, and thirty-seven percent drink to get high.

Since the 1950s, the American Medical Association has defined alcoholism as a primary disease; that is, it stands by itself and is not just a symptom of something else.[3] Alcoholism, which is influenced by psychosocial and environmental factors, is progressive and fatal. A person who is alcoholic has continuous or periodic impaired control over alcohol. The alcoholic is preoccupied with alcohol, uses it despite consequences, and tends to live in denial about what is going on. While the majority of people in our society

---

[3] It is important to note the difference between alcohol abuse and alcohol dependency. Alcohol abuse is the overuse of alcohol for a specific period of time, with physical and social consequences. Compulsivity, however, is absent in alcohol abuse. In alcohol dependency, on the other hand, the person has a compulsive need for alcohol, and is less in control.

can "take or leave" alcoholic beverages, the alcoholic becomes compulsively hooked on them.[4]

Youth workers need to be aware of the symptoms of alcohol abuse and alcohol dependency in order to network with professionals in helping young people with such problems. Youth workers also need to be aware of the dynamics of alcoholic families. In a small intergenerational faith group, the teen members may be not "using or abusing" alcohol themselves. But they may be part of families where other members are addicted to alcohol.[5] Claudia Black and others have highlighted for us the roles some young people play in such families: *the hero,* who is excessively responsible and successful; *the scapegoat,* who often acts out or defies authority in an attempt to divert attention away from the chemically dependent person; *the lost child,* who often is lonely, isolated, and withdrawn; and *the mascot,* who uses charm and humor to defend against painful family dynamics. Aware youth ministers can also see these roles being played out in youth groups and social events.

Suicide

The suicide rate among adolescents has grown over three hundred percent in the last two decades. In fact, accidental death, suicide, and homicide are the top three killers of adolescents today. Between five thousand and six thousand young people take their lives each year. Only fifteen percent to thirty percent of those in suicidal crisis are mentally ill. Three times more females attempt suicide than males, but males complete the act of suicide three times more frequently than females.

The key characteristics of a young person (or anyone, for that matter) in suicidal crisis are hopelessness and helplessness. Teens who contemplate suicide usually have equally strong desires within them to live and to die. For this reason, the suicidal person almost always gives "warning signs" before attempting suicide. Some rather typical warning signs include threats about

---

[4] Alcoholics also run a high risk of addiction to other mood-altering substances. This phenomenon, in which an individual compulsively uses more than one substance, is called "cross-addiction."

[5] The classic unspoken rules of alcoholic and dysfunctional families include these: Don't talk, and the situation will pass; don't feel; don't trust; you should do . . . ; and keep the rules rigid, so that we can survive with each other.

killing oneself, talk about wanting to die, previous attempts at suicide, sudden changes in behavior (withdrawal from others, moodiness, or apathy), depression or crying, making final arrangements (i.e., giving away personal objects), alcohol/drug abuse, feeling and/or using the vocabulary of being unwanted, and tendencies toward violence.

Some factors that may precipitate a suicide crisis include the following:

- *Developmental problems.* Adolescence is a time of high stress. With underdeveloped coping skills, some young people obsess about suicide during problem times.
- *Depression.* Some depression is endogenous, a chronic disease. Some depression can also be transitory and reactive to specific situations.
- *Poor problem-solving skills.* This lack of skills results in tunnel vision, seeing no way out of a problem.
- *Dysfunctional relationships.* Family or peers can be causes of pain and difficulty.
- *Separation from, or loss of, a loved one or object.* No matter how apparently insignificant, the pain of loss is real.
- *Familial disorganization.* The demise of family structures, especially through divorce, renders many young people "lost at sea."
- *Glorification of violence in the media.* Often, death and violence are glorified by the media. Suicide is perceived as one way to gain attention. Death/violence does not seem permanent in the media; one can "come back from it."
- *Loss of hope.* To the degree anyone sees only bleakness in the future, there is the danger of suicidal crisis.

Youth workers can best help young people deal with the issue of suicide by developing skills in prevention, intervention, and postvention.

Prevention. While some parents fear that talking about suicide can bring on suicide attempts, it has been my experience that talking about suicide with young people is liberating. The fact is: The possibility of suicide flashes across the imagination of almost everyone who has been depressed in some way. Having others share how they have dealt with the thoughts of suicide can reassure a young person that he or she is not crazy. Talking with teens about suicide in the context of discussions about all types of self-destructive behaviors is also helpful. Such discussions help to "intellectualize" the issue of suicide.

Intervention. If a young person is depressed or exhibits other warning signs listed in this chapter, it is important that the youth worker accurately access the young person's degree of risk for suicide. This means talking to the young person and listening to what he or she has to say. It means asking questions and hearing the answers. For example, actually ask the questions, "Do you ever consider suicide?" or "How often does suicide cross your mind?" Ask about the possible method the teen would use. (Details about method show an advanced degree of planning, and hence, a greater risk.) Also explore the degree of psychological upheaval. How disturbed does the young person appear to be? It is important not to panic. It is also important not to enter into covenants of secrecy with the possibly suicidal person. Instead, network with parents, guardians, and professionals in an effort to provide immediate help.

Postvention. Often it falls to the pastoral worker to counsel teens and to help them find meaning after a tragedy, such as suicide, has occurred. Throughout my years in youth ministry, several teens did kill themselves. Their deaths had a profound effect on the other teens. I found it very important to gather the teens so that they could express their feelings, remember the person who had died, and pray for healing. Moralizing sermons are not too effective at this time. Instead, it is a time to be together, to grieve, and to share faith. Above all, suicide needs to be deglamorized in order to discourage copycat suicides (a growing phenomenon around the country).

Sexual Activity

One's sexuality is one's self. We are our maleness and femaleness. Because it is so foundational to life, human sexuality needs to be part of youth ministry efforts. Many high school programs offered by schools or other agencies focus too much on the mechanical or biological factors of sex. A ministerial setting, however, allows young people to discuss the feelings, values, attitudes, morality, and spirituality that are also part of sexuality.

In the 1980s, Robert Coles and Geoffrey Stokes interviewed over one thousand adolescents in forty-nine states. In their book *Sex and the American Teenager,* they published their findings:

- Over half the males and females interviewed had sexual intercourse by age eighteen.
- Most adolescents said that loves gives one permission to have sexual intercourse, but they could not describe what love is.
- Two-thirds of those interviewed said they would not marry their most recent sex partner.
- Peer pressure (sharing sexual escapades with "the guys") and fear ("He won't ask me out again") were the biggest motivators toward sexual activity.
- Combined with growing sexual activity among teens is the lack of fundamental sexual knowledge.
- Abortion among teens is epidemic and is being used as just another birth control device.
- Teen pregnancies are epidemic.
- The age of starting sexual activity is becoming younger and younger, now in the preadolescent range.
- Only a small fraction of the teens interviewed said that religion had any influence on their sexual activity.

A more recent publication, entitled *The U.S. Youth Risk Behavior Study,* indicates that fewer than half of the sexually active high school students use a condom during sex. Such teens are not only risking an unwanted pregnancy; they are also risking the possibility of infection with the HIV virus.

One of the strategies I have used in discussing human sexuality with young people is to nudge the discussion away from genitality to sexuality. Genitality is a preoccupation with body parts and their use. "Safe sex" discussions often focus on genitality—the use of body parts in such a way that there will not be the conception of a child or the transmission of the HIV virus. In discussing human sexuality, however, young people must suddenly confront issues such as identity, communication, intimacy, commitment, and responsibility.

Making human sexuality, rather than genitality, the center of discussion has several advantages. First, sexual morality can be presented as learning a discernment process regarding how best and most responsibly to use the gift of one's sexuality. Second, a new positive approach to chastity can be emphasized; chastity can be defined as responsible use of human sexuality, reverencing the other's and one's own sexuality and seeing physical expressions of affection as part of a continuum of communication and commitment. Third, marriage and family life can be retrieved as sacred institutions in which the fullness of human sexuality can be experienced and celebrated.

A human sexuality issue of which I am just becoming aware is ministry to gay young people. As a recent study revealed, a significant number of attempted adolescent suicides are among young people who are wrestling with questions about their sexual orientation.[6] Because of this concern, the Horizons Community Center, in the Lakeview neighborhood of Chicago, has established a service for homosexual teens. Under the leadership of adult advisors, gay and lesbian young people, as well as young people wrestling with issues of sexual orientation, can share their pain, ask questions, and receive support. People in orientation confusion who discover that they are heterosexual are taught not to criticize those who remain on for help with their homosexuality.[7] While Catholic youth ministry centers might not want to adopt a full-blown ministry to gay teens as Horizons does, homosexuality and homophobia are two topics that should be included in broader discussions with teens about human sexuality.[8]

Rock Music and Pop Culture

Although aging may bring with it an aversion to rock music and pop culture, there is no way to do youth evangelization or ministry without having both an awareness of and an exposure to these phenomena. Listening to rock music and trying to understand the meaning of young people's music is an important step toward entering their world. It is also an important step toward helping young people listen to and look at pop culture critically—

[6] The U.S. Department of Health and Human Services says that gay and lesbian adolescents are two to three times as likely to attempt suicide than their heterosexual counterparts.

[7] If the media is any barometer of what is going on in young people's lives, this issue of homosexual teens may be "coming out of the closet." Recent episodes of the highly rated daily drama *One Life to Live* unfolded the story of sixteen-year-old Billy Douglas as he came to grips with and admitted his gay orientation.

[8] Unfortunately, recent Vatican pronouncements about homosexuality, particularly judgmental and punitive in tone, have been partially detrimental to young people who are struggling with the issue of sexual orientation.

to discern what is of Christ and our tradition, and what is anti-Gospel or anti-Christ.

Journalist Richard Corliss, in the May 7, 1990, edition of *Time* magazine, asks whether the 1990s are destined to be the "Filth Decade." In an article entitled "X-Rated," Corliss lists some of the people and groups who push the boundaries of decency in their performing: Andrew Dice Clay, Motley Crue, The Beastie Boys, 2 Live Crew, Howard Stern, Ozzy Osbourne, N.W.A. (Niggers with an Attitude), Eddie Murphy, and Guns N' Roses. In an earlier editorial in *Newsweek* magazine of May 6, 1985, Randy Stroud published a similar list that included the names of Prince, Sheena Easton, Madonna, Judas Priest, and W.A.S.P. It is true that such performers affect and influence young people. As Aristotle once wrote, "Music has the power to form character." Dr. Joseph Novello (the director of a Washington, D.C., drug program) says that a young person's musical taste—satanic, sexual, drug-related, etc.—definitely reveals something about the state of his or her mind.[9]

In "A Parent's View of Pop Sex and Violence" (*Time*, May 7, 1990), Charles Alexander isolates the issue well: Too much of today's entertainment carries messages that are dangerous to society. Among these messages are the following three: Women are sexual objects to be used and abused by men; violence is an effective means of resolving conflicts; and it is all right to hate another class of people. Tipper Gore, founder of the Parents' Music Resource Center, concurs with Alexander. She estimates that at least fourteen million young people are "at risk" because of the negative impact of the media.

I think youth workers need to be interested in rock music and pop culture for three reasons. First, the teens themselves are interested in it. Second, some inherent messages of rock music and pop culture contradict Christian values; in order to counter these messages, we need to know what they are. And third, teens are being financially exploited; this is a situation that, in justice, needs to be stopped.

Youth workers should keep in mind that there are major themes that run through much of rock music: being "cool," friendship, relationships (love,

---

[9] The comments of Corliss, Stroud, Aristotle, and Novello—while serious in themselves—do not even include the huge amount of pornographic genital activity and violence present in movies and on television today.

sexuality, loss), social criticism, escape through chemicals or sexual activity, celebration, pressure, freedom, and facing an unknown future. Through these themes, given songs can be life-enhancing, life-degrading, or mixed. In any case, the songs should not be taken at face value; young people need to be taught how to analyze the lyrics.

Some helpful questions youth workers can ask young people in presenting a song for analysis include the following:
* Do you like the song? Why or why not?
* How does the song make you feel?
* What does the song urge you to do, say, or believe?
* What is the main theme of the song?
* What is the main message of the song?
* Is the message in line with what we, as Christians, believe? If so, why? If not, why not?

It is always important for the youth worker, ahead of time, to listen to and reflect on the song.

Eating Disorders

Among young people, the two most prevalent eating disorders are bulimia and anorexia. After five years of research with young adults, Marlene Boskind-White and William White, Jr., coined the term "bulimarexia" (bulimia and anorexia). In the late 1970s, Marlene noticed a pattern among many of her adolescent and young adult female patients: Although most of them were thin, they never thought they were thin enough. Most had low-grade depression; many also had anxiety symptoms, and many reported being lonely and uprooted in relationships. Many of these young women openly admitted to orgy-like binges in which they stuffed themselves with food. After a binge, they would purge themselves through vomiting or laxatives.

Boskind-White and White targeted the adolescent/young adult years as crucial in the development of bulimarexia. Indeed, this cyclical eating disorder is epidemic in American society, affecting mostly women from the teen years to mid-life.[10] The eating disorder reaches its fullest fruition when

---

[10] Without doubt, the media have played a central role in promoting bulimarexia. The media, on the one hand, hold up female slenderness as a cultural icon. On the other hand, the media promote the intake of high caloric junk food.

the bulimarexic believes the binge-purge dynamics are the truest parts of her identity. Although the binge-purge cycles are often both found in the same person, one pattern of symptoms may stand out over other symptoms in one individual. That is, some people tend to binge more; others tend to fast and purge more. Thus, among people with bulimarexia, some are anorexic, some are bulimic, and some are a hybrid. Young women suffering with bulimarexia are often from middle-class, upwardly mobile families, where the mother tends to be overly involved in her daughter's life, and the father is absent or overly involved in work outside the home.

Whether the person leans toward binging and purging or toward fasting, the dynamics are the same. These rituals are secretive. Bulimarexics suffer from poor body image. The ritualistic behaviors help them to postpone activity, to avoid possible failure, to reduce the stress of social encounters, to postpone sexual intimacy, to get revenge on people who are perceived as having hurt them, or to produce a feeling of control over chaotic life situations. The physiological results of binging and purging include hypoglycemia, metabolic changes, neurological changes, physical changes, and mood/psychological changes. Group therapy, with peer support and challenge, often seems to be more effective than individual therapy in treating this disorder.

A Reminder

With eating disorders—as with all the youth issues and needs discussed in this chapter—the youth worker is not expected to be the "firing-line" expert or professional. He or she, however, should be sensitive to the symptoms of these problems and should always be ready to network with professionals for help. The youth worker should also be willing to communicate and work with parents—the topic of the next chapter.

— 12 —

The Missing Piece: Ministry to Parents

Charles Fisherman, a psychiatrist and family therapist, believes that one of the great challenges facing family life in the future is teaching parents and their teens how to talk to one another. Often, parents ask questions or make statements that can be invasive, passive aggressive, or sarcastic in nature. Similarly, teens tend to answer questions with monosyllabic responses that basically tell the adult world, "Mind your own business!" One therapist compared parent-teen communications as equivalent to leaving messages on each other's voice recorders. What is really going on is a power game. Parents and teens are both trying to show the other how they are in charge of the relationship.

Although the title of this chapter targets parents, in reality, both teens and parents need training in bridging each other's world. Teens need to be taught to share with their parents at least part of what happened to them during their day. If practiced, this could be a very nonthreatening way to stay in touch with parents and reveal what it is like to be a young person today. Parents, in turn, need to be encouraged to ask questions of their teens, in a tone that is not indicting or cynical. Both parents and teens have to learn to spend time with each other—not in artificial ways, but maximizing the time they already have together at meals, in the kitchen, out driving in the car. Since most of this book has addressed the development of skills by adolescents and young adults, we will spend this chapter reflecting on skills that parents need to develop.

I critique much of my early efforts at youth ministry as being "segregationalist." The teams and I segregated youth, in part, from the adult world. This did little to bridge the worlds of teens and adults; it did little to facilitate advocacy for teens to the adult world. In more recent years, the value of also involving parents as targets of the total youth ministry effort (getting teens and parents together for education and simple sharing) has become apparent to me. Youth ministry needs to provide alternative familial groups like FLAME communities. It needs also to help heal "the clan."

Parenting Training

Parenting training has had an evolution here in America. The Adlerian school of psychology, under the leadership of Rudolf Dreikers, put parenting training on the map in the 1950s. In the late 1960s and early 1970s, Thomas Gordon popularized parenting skills in written form. This gradually became known as STEP, or Systematic Training in Effective Parenting. In the 1980s and 1990s, Dr. Michael Popkin translated the essential vision and skills of STEP into the contemporary idiom, placing much of his work on videocassette for use in the home or in groups.

Dolores Curran, in *Stress and the Healthy Family*, states that parents need to be aware that some stress is an inevitable part of family living. Healthy families accept that fact, minimize toxic stress, and do their best always to resolve conflicts. The "well-stressed" family makes the time for conflict resolution, shared family customs, and shared religious traditions.

In *The Missing Link* (which was already mentioned), Richard Schectman identifies "the missing link" in most families with the lack of quality time parents or guardians spend with their teens. Parents, Schectman says, need to assess their relationship with their teens, grieve the loss of certain kinds of closeness that were present in childhood, realize that the teens are going through periods of value reassessment and shifting, and take on the role of "consultant" to their teens. Schectman says, in terms of interpersonal dynamics, that uninvolved adults contribute to the uninvolvement or underinvolvement of teens in the family. On the other hand, overinvolved parents contribute to the creation of overinvolved, clinging teens. Adversary parents contribute to the adversarial stance that some teens adopt toward the adult world. Likewise, cooperative, encouraging parents contribute to cooperative, encouraged teens.

When I am asked to facilitate effective parenting workshops, these are some of the skills I emphasize:

- *Active listening.* Parents need to break through a teen's often-encoded messages to name and reflect back what the teen is communicating. In addition to content, parents also need to listen to the feelings the teen is communicating.

- *Empathy and confrontation.* Parents need to use "I feel" statements and avoid "you" put-down statements in order to challenge teens without impugning their character.

- *Conflict resolution.* Parents need to incorporate "win-win" strategies when communicating with teens. They need to learn how to resolve conflicts with no one walking away with a sense of having lost.

- *Democratic families.* Parents often "set the environment" in the home. Instead of creating an environment of anarchy, parents need to encourage an atmosphere in which the rights of all family members are respected.

- *Encouragement.* Parents must learn to affirm and encourage what is good in their teens.

- *Consequences.* Parents need to learn not to save their teens from the consequences of their poor choices—unless, of courses, those consequences are life-threatening.

- *Detachment from problematic behavior.* Parents need to be able to deal with problematic behavior in their teens, but also maintain a certain distance. In other words, they can't let a teen's negative behavior determine or control their own responses.

- *Time together.* Parents need to retrieve a healthy sense of play in teens by spending leisure time together.

- *Family councils.* Parents, with children and teens, need to carve into their schedules one sacred time per week when the family gathers for discussion of rules, tone of the family, plans, schedules, etc.

In short, I believe that ministry to parents should, in some way, be incorporated into full-cycle youth ministry. At times, the parents need to be in small groups by themselves. At other times, parents and teens should be together in small groups. While these structures are still in need of evolution, they will uphold certain values: mutual respect between teens and adults, cooperation, and shared spiritual values.

How to Do All of This?

By now, you are probably wondering how one parish could possibly do everything I have suggested in this book. The truth is: It can't. What I believe is needed in the future is regionalized youth ministry. The next chapter will develop this idea more fully.

— 13 —

Regionalized Youth Ministry

We live in a Church of diminishing resources. On the one hand, the pool of clergy and "professional" religious is becoming smaller. On the other hand, we are just now awakening to the rich possibilities of baptismal spirituality—the call to ministry and holiness that is shared by all the baptized. I do not think we have yet learned how to tap into the rich resource of our lay people. We have not yet learned how to unleash lay people for mission, to utilize their already empowered-by-the-Spirit personalities.

One thing I am becoming sure of is this: Each parish can no longer afford to "reinvent the wheel." Some ministries and pastoral services (especially youth ministry) can best be done by parishes who pool together their resources to hire competent, skilled professionals. These professionals, in turn, will animate people from the various parishes who discern that they are gifted for youth ministry. With the plethora of real estate and vacant buildings that the Catholic Church owns—schools, rectories, convents, etc.—space could be created for a regional youth ministry center.[1]

I think one of the reasons the evangelical youth movements are successful is that they are not geographically bound, as most parishes are.

---

[1] My first extensive, full-time work with young people involved changing an old convent into a youth ministry center for the whole town. The center was used for recreation, religious education sessions, nights of renewal, and retreats. The building's evolution and use were truly a wonderful experience.

Rather, the evangelicals see themselves as ministering to a far-flung area, an area that would encompass many "parishes." I believe that if Catholic parishes would add geographic expansiveness to the dynamics of full-cycle youth ministry and the principles of maximum influence and multiplication, we would have a youth evangelization effort that is truly missionary in nature.

Regionalized youth ministry must include the renewed vision of the youth minister as a "coordinator" of youth ministries. The director of a youth ministry center should "animate" and train other adults and teens for ministry to youth. If the ministry expands (as it should if it follows the principles in this book), other professionals will have to be hired to coordinate the main pieces of ministry to youth: Scripture, worship, mentoring and spiritual direction, social ministry, outreach, ministry to troubled youth, etc.

This may sound like a "pie in the sky" idea, but I am hoping pastoral staffs will give the concept serious thought. While some parishes—here and there—are doing good things for youth, the Catholic Church, on average, is missing its young people. Many young people, even if they still attend Mass, go elsewhere (especially to evangelical groups) for nurturance and fellowship.[2]

Unfortunately, despite all our recent verbiage over the quintacentennial anniversary of evangelization in the Americas, not much has changed to better youth ministry or to appreciate the richness that young people bring to the Church. If the Church continues the status quo, it runs the risk of losing generations of young people for centuries. The nominal Catholic of the future is not going to be the person still stung by *Humanae Vitae* or hurt by a priest or pastoral worker. No, the nominal Catholic of the future is today's young person who is bored with a Church in maintenance, does not feel part of the increasingly graying, aging Church, and does not feel that Church leaders are even aware of his or her real concerns and problems.

Granted, parishes will have to let go of parochialism and competition in order to move toward regionalized youth ministry. For this reason, both

---

[2] Allan Figueroa Deck, in his book *The Second Wave,* expresses similar sentiments regarding the Church's evangelization of recent immigrants. Deck believes the Church is failing to evangelize its second wave of immigrants—especially Asians and Hispanics. He warns that if the Church loses these people to the evangelical groups or to indifference, we will have lost them for centuries.

in my writing and my talks, I have been encouraging clusters of parishes to reimagine themselves as "pastoral alliances for excellence." In such alliances, the main concerns are "the customer" (young people) and an excellent "product" (ministry to youth). Of course, pastoral alliances for excellence can be broadened to include any demographic group of "customers" and a variety of "products." The key paradigm shift in this line of thinking is away from competitive, maintenance ministry to cooperative, collaborative, mission-oriented ministry.

Obviously, regionalized youth ministry programs cannot run on prayers and goodwill alone. Finances will be needed. That is why now is the time for pastoral leaders to challenge adults (most especially parents) to be generous in financing youth evangelization ministry efforts. Young people, too, should be challenged to contribute, however little it may be, to youth and other evangelization efforts. These efforts should happen, not because teens are the future of the Church, but because they are the needy, wounded Church NOW. Young people have a baptismal right to excellent ministry—to receive it and then to share and give it to each other and the larger Church. How we spend our money reflects our values. Whether we emotionally and financially invest in young people has, and will continue to have, a profound impact on the quality of our Church.

14

What Kind of Church?
What Kind of World?

A s I mentioned earlier, in her book *Beyond Therapy, Beyond Science,* Ann Wilson Schaef says that each of us has processes going on deep within us. A deep process is a profound life movement, often begun earlier in life, and advancing into the present. As I mentioned earlier, tears, spontaneous memories, dreams, repetitively hummed songs, and other rather common experiences are often doorways into our deep processes. According to Schaef, it is important for us to explore our deep processes and not to resist them, so that we might learn from them and be healed.

Just as individuals grow by journeying through deep processes, so the Church experiences similar growth. Today's Church is certainly in the midst of a deep process, rooted in the past and profoundly influenced by ecclesial and cultural events of the last few decades. What is crucial to note, I believe, is that there is always resistance on the part of some Church members (leaders and lay people) to enter into the deep process. Such people try to repress, sedate, or tranquilize the deep process. Such denial and resistance to growth is not necessarily healthy. For as Ann Schaef points out, any deep process that is denied and resisted will go underground, only to recycle and emerge as a more painful experience later.

Gerald Arbuckle, in *Change, Grief, and Renewal in the Church,* speaks of grief—both individual and corporate—as a necessary prologue to change.

Not to grieve is to deny the fact of death. Arbuckle contends that death—with the possibility of growth and new life—abounds in the Church. Yet many Catholics refuse to grieve; they deny the deep process of change. True grieving involves some anger, depression, and wandering; but eventually the grieving person lets go and moves on. As Arbuckle says, grieving as a Church will free us to refound the Church around innovative pastoral strategies needed to effect good evangelization. Arbuckle's concept of evangelization has little to do with acquiring greater numbers of people. Rather, he sees it as the radical call to gospel living, to conversion, and to moving into the world with a sense of mission.

The Future Church

I believe that if we, as Church, work through our "deep processes" and do true "grieving," we will let the Spirit lead us toward a future where we develop positive structures and strategies that fit the Church's mission to usher in the Reign of God—a reality in which people live God-centered lives in communion with each other and with a sense of justice for all. Hopefully, the Church's future will be characterized by a strong adult faith, rather than the "tail wagging the dog" (that is, ministry to children steering the course of parish life). By budgeting more of its resources for adult and family forms of religious education, the Church I envision will give special emphasis to young adult ministry, to ministry to mid-lifers, and to better ministry to the burgeoning senior citizen population.

I also believe the Church will become more of a "community of communities." The large liturgical assembly will be a gathering of small *Koinonia*-type groups and the domestic churches experienced at home. Ministry itself will become more collaborative. Serious attention will be given to the discernment of giftedness—helping all the baptized discern how they have been gifted and what is God's call to ministry in their lives. As a result, more of the baptized will awaken to mission and ministry. In our parishes, there will be fewer people in the "audience" and more on the "team."

Correspondingly, the role of presbyter will change drastically. Priests will become presiders and pastoral/theological consultants to clusters of parishes. Parishes will be run by directors of pastoral life, business administrators, and communities of ministers (Scripture, worship, pastoral care, youth ministry, etc.). The pastoring, or shepherding, of each group of ten to fifteen households in the parish will be given to trained laity. Regular events of a healing and reconciling nature will be held in clusters of parishes to attract and welcome both nominal Catholics and members of the other Christian churches.

The schooling, content-oriented approach to religious education will not be "saved by the bell" of *Catechism of the Catholic Church*. Instead, the Spirit will continue to nudge us toward more lectionary-based, Eucharist-based, family- and home-oriented kinds of efforts. The goal for religious education programs will continue to be "the gradual initiation of people of all ages into community."

Likewise, Catholic devotional life will, of necessity, develop services of healing for the multiple layers of woundedness in society (addictions, divorce, unemployment, physical illness, emotional illness, etc.). In other words, devotion will wed the "transcendent" with the real world. Education and ministry will prepare the baptized for responsible citizenship, global consciousness, and the transformation of society into God's Reign.

I believe that women in the Church will continue to lead with existential authority. Communion services will replace Eucharist as the norm for many Catholics across the land. Deprivation of the Eucharist will motivate many Catholics to demand the use of married clergy, who can make Eucharist more available.

Guilt and obligation will cease to be motivations for church attendance. Beginning with the current young adult population, people will vote with their feet; they will go to churches where they are spiritually nourished. As a result, the Church will learn from the business world the importance of learning from the best, even if "the best" is found "in the competition." Ineffective, paper-bound downtown-supervised structures will become grass-roots, pastoral alliances for excellence in ministry.

Finally, it will become increasingly clear to us that everything the Church and parishes and evangelization are about is intimately connected to justice. More of us will become more prayerful about, and involved in, justice issues.

Some Last Thoughts

I want to conclude by borrowing a metaphor from Sally Cunneen in her book *Mother Church*. "Mother Church" is leaving. The torch of the Reign of God, which she has jealously grasped in her institutional hands, is finally being passed to the *laos theou,* the People of God. My predictions about the future simply reflect my belief that these are some of the directions where the Spirit is moving us. It is in this future Church that our young people will hopefully minister and flourish. Let us not try to abort the deep process of change. Let us not make the pain worse by trying to anesthetize grief. In fact, we owe it to Mother Church to pass on the richness of the Church to our young people and their children. The richness will be a synthesis of ancient tradition and innovative pastoral approaches and expressions of the ever-new Good News.